$\Leftarrow\Rightarrow$

Zero-deposit

Competition => Bypass

to tenants => commission to

Zero deposit

Self insurance

£850 => indent...

Lendlord => miles on the road

Advances in Monetary Policy Design

Advances in Monetary Policy Design: Applications to the Gulf Monetary Union

By

William A. Barnett and Ryadh M. Alkhareif

CAMBRIDGE SCHOLARS PUBLISHING

Advances in Monetary Policy Design: Applications to the Gulf Monetary Union,
by William A. Barnett and Ryadh M. Alkhareif

This book first published 2013

Cambridge Scholars Publishing

12 Back Chapman Street, Newcastle upon Tyne, NE6 2XX, UK

British Library Cataloguing in Publication Data
A catalogue record for this book is available from the British Library

ISBN (10): 1-4438-4829-8, ISBN (13): 978-1-4438-4829-9

CONTENTS

List of Tables

LIST OF FIGURES

ABSTRACT

In the aftermath of the 2007-08 financial crisis when the short-term nominal interest rate reached zero, many central banks worldwide have adopted unconventional monetary policy tools such as quantitative easing where central banks inject money via purchases of long-term government bonds to stimulate their economies. Using the officially published simple-sum monetary aggregates to measure monetary service flows of the economy can be misleading since the simple-sum index ignores the liquidity characteristics of assets in monetary aggregates. Divisia indexes remove the investment motive and measure all other monetary services associated with economic liquidity, by allowing the weights of monetary assets to vary depending on their monetary services at the margin. This book introduces key economic indicators for the Gulf states and discusses the main issues related to monetary policy and theory, aggregation theory and index number theory. It outlines the methods for constructing proper inflation and monetary indexes that are consistent with monetary theory and aggregation theory. Moreover, it provides guidelines for creating optimal monetary aggregation, as suggested by the originator of Divisia monetary aggregation, William A. Barnett.

This book reports on the first Divisia monetary aggregates for the complete GCC area and focuses on economic measurement. The second chapter builds monthly time-series of Divisia monetary aggregates for the Gulf area for the period of June 2004 to December 2011, using area-wide data. It also offers an "economic stability" indicator for the GCC area by analyzing the dynamics pertaining to certain variables such as the dual price aggregates, aggregate interest rates, and the Divisia aggregate user-cost growth rates.

Our findings unfold the superiority of the Divisia indexes over the officially published simple-sum monetary aggregates in monitoring the business cycles. There is also direct evidence on higher economic harmonization between GCC countries—especially in terms of their financial markets and the monetary policy. Monetary policy often uses interest rate rules, when the economy is subject only to technology shocks. In that case, money is nevertheless relevant as an endogenous indicator [Woodford, M. (2003). *Interest and Prices: Foundations of a Theory of Monetary Policy*. Princeton, NJ: Princeton University Press]. Properly weighted monetary aggregates provide critical information to policy makers regarding inside liquidity created by financial intermediaries. In addition, policy rules should include money as well as interest rates, when the economy is subject to monetary shocks as well as technology shocks. The data show narrow aggregates growing while broad aggregates collapsed following the financial crises. This information clearly signals problems with the financial system's ability to create liquidity during the crises.

The third chapter investigates the feasibility of forming a common currency area over the Gulf states by testing the weak separability of the monetary aggregates within and then over the GCC countries. Our findings indicate the weak separability of the broad monetary aggregates for the individual GCC countries from private consumption and hence the existence of broad monetary aggregates. The narrow monetary aggregates do exist for the GCC countries except for Qatar where the demand deposits (which offer positive interest rates) cannot be grouped with currency.

Our weak separability tests on the Gulf area confirm the existence of the broad monetary aggregate. However, a narrow monetary aggregate for the entire GCC area does not exist and hence the GCC countries cannot form a common currency area. We find that if Oman is excluded from the monetary union, being a non-oil producing country and hence heterogeneous with respect to the remaining GCC countries, a common currency area is feasible.

Using our admissible groups of GCC monetary assets, we construct Divisia monetary aggregates. Our findings suggest the superiority of Divisia indexes over their counterpart simple-sum monetary aggregates in resembling the business cycle patterns where Divisia monetary indexes are low prior to the recent financial crisis and higher afterwards indicating their ability to signal financial turmoil.

Finally, the fourth chapter provides core inflation indicators for the complete GCC area along with alternative inflation measurements. It constructs core inflation indicators for the GCC countries and then recursively builds a single core inflation indicator for the Gulf area for the period of June 2004 to December 2011. This chapter proposes core inflation indicators for the GCC area based upon two alternative monetary aggregates: Divisia monetary aggregates and simple-sum monetary aggregates. Using the Generalized Dynamic Factor Model (GDFM), the core inflation indicators for the Gulf area were obtained by extracting the long-term common components of inflation while disregarding the short-term components—thereby eliminating idiosyncratic shocks and transitory noise from our inflation measures. Lastly, this chapter shows that the predictive performance of the Divisia monetary aggregates dominates their simple-sum counterparts for inflation forecasts in the Gulf area.

ACKNOWLEDGEMENTS

We are grateful to Mohammed Al-Kheraif of the Gulf Cooperation Council for supplying financial data, and we thank Mario Forni for valuable comments. The views expressed in this book represent those of the authors and do not necessarily reflect the position of the Saudi Arabian Monetary Agency.

CHAPTER ONE

INTRODUCTION

The goal of this segment is to briefly describe the developments in the Gulf Cooperation Council (GCC) economies with special emphasis on the economic integration between the Gulf countries. We also highlight the role of the GCC countries in the global economy by describing the main economic links of the Gulf countries with the global economy. Finally, we discuss some of the economic prospects as well as the key challenges facing the GCC countries.

1.1. Developments and Economic Integration in the Gulf Area

1.1.1 The Formation of the Gulf Cooperation Council

In 1981, the GCC was established to foster economic growth and strengthen the economic policies for the six Gulf States: Bahrain, Kuwait, Oman, Qatar, Saudi Arabia, and United Arab Emirates (UAE). This supranational institution is effectively the keystone for economic development in the Gulf region where GCC countries resolve critical economic issues that transform the Gulf area toward a more unified economic bloc.

Political stability is a key condition for spurring foreign and domestic investments as well as maintaining sustainable economic growth. One objective of the GCC mutual agreement is to maintain political stability against any possible threat on the Gulf region. To preserve political unity in the Gulf region, the GCC countries have formed a supranational security force—known as the Peninsula Shield Force. In Bahrain, for example, the demonstrations and civil uprisings, for which the government has declared a state of emergency, have led to a sudden downturn in economic activities, especially in the tourism industry. To restore safety in the region and to avoid any foreign intervention in the Gulf territory, the Peninsula Shield Force ensures safety in Bahrain. This is clear evidence that the GCC countries have reached a high level of political integration.

Financial markets and more specifically stock markets are highly integrated between the GCC countries. The GCC countries share similar economic structures and are subject to the same economic shocks. Due to this economic cohesion, the GCC countries have formed a monetary union—known as the Gulf Monetary Council (GMC).

1.1.2 The Establishment of the Gulf Monetary Council

In March 2010, the GMC was established to uniformly implement Gulf-wide monetary policy over all member states. However, Oman and the UAE have opted out of the GMC. Oman has not met the convergence criteria required for joining the union, and the UAE abandoned the union after announcing that the GMC is to be headquartered in Saudi Arabia. These factors have caused the GMC to delay launching the Gulf's single currency. The growing fears inspired by the slowdown of the world economy and more specifically the recession in neighboring European countries led the GMC to postpone circulating the Gulf common currency until 2015.

1.2. Main Characteristics of the GCC Economies

In this part of the introduction, we provide a brief description about the key factors shaping the GCC economies. We also describe the monetary policy as well as the fiscal policy in the Gulf area—with more emphasis on the ties between those sectors and the global economy. Lastly, we provide some information about the trade sector in the Gulf area, since the current account surplus in most of the GCC countries comes from oil exports. Unlike other developing countries, current account balances in the GCC countries have been in a surplus due to the fact that oil revenues directly shape the Gulf economies.

1.2.1 The Real Economy

The Gross domestic product (GDP) growth rates of the GCC countries have closely commoved overtime—implying that the GCC countries are more likely to have synchronized business cycles. The real GDP growth rates of the Gulf countries have been buoyant at around 5% on average, as the demand for natural resources continues to grow (Figure 1-1). Indeed, the economies of the GCC countries are more likely to grow as the world oil-demand is expected to rise. The GCC economies have been expanding as seen in the GDP's largely positive growth rates during the last three decades. At times of economic downturns, the GCC countries were able to recover. In the early 1980s the GCC economies were headed toward a recession as a result of a sudden drop in oil prices. The subsequent rise of oil prices led to a rapid recovery when GDP growth rates rebounded and reached 3% on average. During the Gulf war the economy of Kuwait collapsed and the GDP reached record-low rates (Figure 1-1). Finally, the 2007-08 financial crisis has adversely impacted the GCC economies —especially in the UAE where real estate prices crashed following the government bail out to the largest real estate companies.

Inflation in the Gulf countries seems to be highly correlated with oil prices for which higher oil prices imply higher oil revenues that put an upward pressure on aggregate demand causing higher inflation, and vice versa. Another factor that could affect inflation in the Gulf area comes from the fact that GCC countries, except Kuwait, peg their exchange rates to the U.S. dollar. As the U.S. dollar continues to depreciate, the Gulf national currencies will depreciate as well—causing an inflationary pressure in the Gulf region as the purchasing power of the Gulf currencies deteriorate against major trading partners, mainly the European and Asian countries.

Inflation in the GCC countries has increased during periods of high oil prices. During the 1980s, for example, when oil prices suddenly increased, inflation rates in many GCC countries reached double-digit levels (Figure 1-2). In early to mid-2008 when oil prices surged and reached maximum levels (approximately $120 per barrel) for more than a decade, thereby boosting economic growth in the GCC countries, the inflation rates have soared in the GCC area (Figure 1-2). After the Iraqi invasion in the early 1990s, inflation rates in Kuwait increased and reached double-digit levels (above 15%) as the country underwent massive re-construction projects to rebuild the infrastructure for the country.

Idiosyncratic and sectorial-specific factors have also influenced inflation in the Gulf region. For example, inflation rates in Qatar exceeded 7% as a result of the rapid advancement in the natural gas sector. Prior to the financial crisis, the boom in the real estate sector in Qatar and the UAE explains the higher inflation rates in those countries relative to other GCC countries (Figure 1-2). Although interest rates in GCC countries have been exceptionally low corresponding to those for the U.S. dollar, inflation has been subdued over the last year, where inflation rates have remained below 5%.

In spite of the expansionary fiscal policies in the GCC area that have led to stronger output growth for most of the GCC economies in the past few years, the alarming unemployment rates in some of the GCC countries are problematic. The oil market predominantly drives the GCC economies and hence the government sector has the largest share of employment. As population in the GCC countries increases at a fast pace where the number of job seekers increases correspondingly, job creation is a key challenge for some of the GCC countries. While GCC countries exhibit similar economic structures in which oil transactions account for most of the government revenues, there is a wide disparity between GCC countries' unemployment rates.

In 2006, the unemployment rate exceeded 12% and has been falling since then as the Saudi government initiated various social programs and other government policies to spur job creation in the domestic economy.[1] The unemployment rate has been buoyant at around 10% on average for Saudi Arabia in the past couple of years. The recurring demonstrations in Bahrain have adversely affected the domestic economy where unemployment stands at 15%. Unemployment in Oman displays similar movements to those in Bahrain, since both countries are less reliant on oil income. In Kuwait, unemployment is about 2.5-4%. Finally, unemployment rates in Qatar and the UAE are near 2-3%.[2]

1.2.2 Monetary Policy

With the exception of Kuwait, all the GCC central banks maintain a fixed exchange rate against the U.S. dollar with free capital movements in their countries. The GCC central banks as a result have forgone independence of their monetary policy—suggesting that interest rates in the GCC countries are highly driven by the monetary policy decisions made by the U.S. Federal Reserve. Since maintaining a fixed exchange rate against the U.S. dollar is the policy target in the GCC countries, the GCC central banks have a minor role in steering the domestic economy. Nonetheless, the central banks in the Gulf area can still adopt alternative macroprudential policy tools to control inflation in the Gulf area. By using the macroprudential policy tools effectively, the GCC central banks were able to bring inflation rates back to normal levels (Figure 1-2).

Due to the large current account surpluses associated with windfall oil revenues, the GCC central banks' foreign exchange reserves stand at 10%, on average, of the countries' GDP, with the exception of Saudi Arabia (Table 1-1). As the largest GCC country in terms of GDP, the foreign

---

[1] See the Saudi Arabian Monetary Agency's 48th Annual Report.

[2] For more information about the unemployment in the Gulf area, see the GCC central banks' statistical bulletins.

exchange reserves held by the Saudi central bank, known as the Saudi Arabian Monetary Agency (SAMA), have exceeded $525 billion, which is about 90% of Saudi Arabia's GDP. Table 1-1 shows that the foreign exchange reserves of Saudi Arabia exceeded the country's GDP in 2009. Although a large portion of oil revenues is spent toward various development projects and social programs to improve the economic stance in the domestic economies, most of the GCC countries have built up their international reserves primarily to strengthen monetary policy. Having their currencies fixed against the U.S. dollar, the GCC countries maintain high levels of foreign exchange reserves to limit speculation attacks and stabilize their domestic economies.

The European sovereign debt crisis has deteriorated the balance sheets for many European banks—drying up the lending channels, especially the ones between the European banks and the GCC banks. While many banks in the euro zone have experienced enormous capital shortfalls, domestic banks in the Gulf area have built up sufficient capital buffers to meet the capital requirements initiated in Basel III. The soundness of the banking system in the GCC is exemplified by not only the higher capital adequacy ratios, but also the lower non-performing loan ratios. This implies that the GCC banks' balance sheets remain strong despite the global recession (Table 1-2).

Although the GCC banks' balance sheets remain strong, there is a need for policymakers to address the risks of spillover from the European debt crisis and reduce the banks vulnerabilities to global downturn. The non-performing loan ratios in Bahrain and the UAE have increased since 2009, since these countries are more exposed to the European banking crisis than the remaining GCC countries (Table 1-2). Finally, provisioning rates remain high for most of the GCC countries, and that exemplifies the strength of the Gulf area's banking system (Table 1-2).

1.2.3 Fiscal Policy

Fiscal policy plays a major role in growing the economies of the GCC countries. A large portion of government revenues in the GCC area comes from oil exports. As a result, an increase in oil prices is often accompanied by higher government budget surplus and vice versa. Figure 1-3 depicts the general government balances as a percentage of GDP for the GCC countries. Clearly, the GCC countries enjoy higher budget surpluses, as the global oil demand continues to grow, especially, in emerging Asian markets.

Overall, the government budget for the GCC countries has been in a surplus—allowing the GCC countries to have more fiscal space which is vital for counter-cyclical policy, especially during times of economic downturn. During the financial crisis, a combination of low oil prices and a counter-cyclical policy, have led to higher budget deficits in some of the GCC countries (Figure 1-3). Following the Iraq-Kuwait war, the government budget deficit in Kuwait has increased due to substantial government spending to rebuild the infrastructure in the country. Only a few years after the war, Kuwait managed to rebalance its budget, as the demand for oil increased.

1.2.4 External Developments

The GCC countries have been key players in the global economy via oil exports. In 2012, Saudi Arabia remained one of the largest exporters of oil with daily production of oil reaching 10 million barrels per day. The dependency on oil exports by the GCC countries insinuated the openness of their economies to the global world. To meet the World Trade Organization (WTO) trade agreements, the GCC countries have been liberal in trading goods and services with the rest of the world. As a result, intra-GCC trade has been modest. Imports among GCC countries stand on average at 5-7% of total imports whereas intra-GCC exports accounts for 8-12% of total exports.[3]

The low degree of regional trade is mainly because the GCC countries share similar economic structure where oil revenues are the main source of income. Bahrain and Oman have the highest intra-GCC trade, as they are the most diversified countries in the Gulf area. The intra-GCC trade is expected to rise corresponding to the ongoing development projects and massive government spending on infrastructure intended to diversify the GCC economies.

1.3. The Role of the GCC Countries in the Global Economy

The GCC countries play a major role in the global economy as these countries hold more than 40% of proven global oil reserves and about 22% for the natural gas. Oil production in the GCC area stands at 23% of global oil production—signifying the pivotal role the GCC countries play in the

[3] See the GCC central banks' statistical bulletins and the International Financial Statistics (IFS).

global economy.[4] Four of the GCC countries, namely, Kuwait, Qatar, Saudi Arabia, and the UAE, are members of the Organization of the Petroleum Exporting Countries (OPEC), which supplies more than 40% of the world's oil production and about 75% of the world's total proven crude oil reserves. The GCC economies depend heavily on oil production to the extent that the GCC countries have become more interconnected to the rest of the world via trade channels and capital account channels.

To smooth government expenditure and further diversify their economies, the GCC countries have invested a large portion of oil revenues in various sovereign wealth funds (SWFs). The International Monetary Fund (IMF) has estimated that the size of the SWFs of the GCC countries has exceeded one trillion dollars. In the UAE, the size of the SWFs owned by Abu Dhabi Investment Authority and Abu Dhabi Investment Council alone stands at $626 billion. The Saudi Arabian Monetary Agency (SAMA) invests about $533 billion in different forms of SWFs. In Kuwait and Qatar, the SWFs are about $296 and $115 billion, respectively [see, e.g., the GCC central banks]. The rapid growth of the SWFs is an indication of stronger integration between the GCC countries and the global economy.

Economic integration in the Gulf region has increasingly gained a momentum manifested in the decision by the GCC countries to join global economic organizations. Saudi Arabia is currently a member of the group of twenty finance ministers and central bank governors—known as the G-20. Collectively, the size of the G-20 economies accounts for more than 80% of the gross world production—signifying the influential role these countries have on the global market and more importantly the financial markets. Moreover, Saudi Arabia and the remaining GCC countries have an affiliation with the IMF. Saudi Arabia is ranked the eighth in voting power at the IMF with about 3% out of total votes. This reflects the significant economic role Saudi Arabia plays in the global economy. Finally, having an affiliation with the World Trade Organization (WTO), the GCC countries have established a strong economic relationship with their trading partners.

1.4. Prospects and Challenges

The GCC economies have benefited from the significant revenue windfall associated with the oil-price hikes in amplifying the fiscal space. Most of the GCC countries were able to run counter-cyclical policies

---

[4] See the OPEC's World Oil Outlook publications.

during the recent financial crisis by using the oil income. In addition, the soundness of the GCC banking system has increased due to the increase in the capital adequacy ratio and a simultaneous decrease in the non-performing loan ratios. The IMF estimated that the GCC economies will continue expanding, as global oil demand's upward trajectory is expected to continue throughout 2015.

Despite the strong growth outlook for most of the GCC economies, a profound structural reform is necessary to sustain economic growth and increase the competitiveness of the GCC economies in the global marketplace. In the following subsection, we discuss the core policy challenges confronting GCC countries including issues related to unemployment, income diversification, and statistics. We focus on these challenges as they form a key systemic challenge to the Gulf countries. We refer readers to the IMF country reports for a more thorough discussion.

1.4.1 Unemployment Challenge

Unemployment rates have reached double-digit numbers in some GCC countries—imposing a serious threat on the welfare of future generations. There are two main factors that have led to the unemployment problem in the GCC countries: (i) the fast population growth, and (ii) insufficient progress in terms of diversifying their economies and job creation.

To reduce unemployment in the Gulf area, policymakers must address these issues and take the necessary steps to turn this problem to their advantage, since most of the unemployed are young (most of them are between 20-29). Instead of focusing on short-term solutions such as expanding the unemployment benefits by funding different social programs, the GCC governments must redirect their investments toward more sustainable projects that can lead to higher job creation rates and add more value to the domestic economy.

The positive externality resulting from building a better infrastructure and investing in capital expenditure projects will reduce unemployment in the Gulf region. Finally, the private sector ought to be more efficient and competitive to attract skilled employees. Of course, this leads to another issue which is about strengthening the link between education institutions' outcomes and jobs' requirements. Governmental officials must bridge the gap between the universities' outcomes and the private sector.

1.4.2 Diversification

Associated with the strong global oil demand is a higher standard of living and economic development in the Gulf countries. In contrast, a decline in oil prices would have an adverse effect on GCC economies, since oil revenues are largely the main source of income. To reduce their reliance on oil production as the main source of income, the GCC countries have reached a pronounced degree of diversification. Since more than 79% of the Saudi population is under 40 years old and about 36% are younger than 15 years old, Saudi Arabia has invested heavily in human capital.[5] In the past few years, the number of universities and other educational institutions has tripled and the amount spent on education has increased to accommodate the growing population of students. Moreover, the Saudi government has issued record-high scholarships to study abroad for more than 130,000 Saudi students with an estimated cost of $2.5 billion, as indicated by the ministry of higher education.

The UAE has spent billions of dollars on advancing the tourism sector, which attracts a large number of tourists from all around the world. In the past couple of years, for example, the number of overseas visitors stands at around eight million on average [see, e.g., the Department of Tourism and Commerce Marketing]. The continuing effort to improve the tourism industry has transformed the UAE, mainly Dubai, to become one of the world's most popular travel destinations.

In Qatar, a massive investment in natural gas and hydrocarbon explorations has increased the country's competitiveness in the global market. In Bahrain, Kuwait, and Oman, advancement in the banking sector and financial innovations has strengthened the countries' financial sector. Tourism also plays an important role in Bahrain and Oman, as they are less reliant on oil income. The degree of diversification in the GCC countries as a result is expected to increase in a faster pace as the economies of these countries shifts more form the oil sector to other industries.

1.4.3 Statistics: Timeliness and Quality of National Data

A major problem facing policymakers at the Gulf Monetary Council (GMC) is the lack of macroeconomic statistics for the GCC area. The scarcity of data has limited economic researchers from exploring the

---

[5] See the Central Department of Statistics and Information for more details.

economic dynamics in the GGG area. The GMC ought to have sufficient data at its disposal to maintain a more vigilant outlook for the economy. Being the central monetary authority in the Gulf area, the GMC seeks to scrutinize many national data and collectively produces a GCC-wide database for the Gulf monetary policy.

As an effort to enhance the quality of statistics in the Gulf area, we provide financial and monetary statistics pertaining to the GCC countries individually and for the whole Gulf union. Our statistics are derived using statistical index number theory and hence consistent with monetary aggregation theory and microeconomic aggregation theory. More specifically, we produce Divisia monetary aggregates for the GCC countries and recursively construct GCC-wide monetary aggregates. Divisia indexes are known for their ability to track the unknown aggregator functions of economic theory as long as these functions are consistent with rational economic behavior. For more information about aggregation theory and Divisia quantity and price indexes, we recommend reading William A. Barnett's latest book "Getting It Wrong: How Faulty Monetary Statistics Undermine the Fed, the Financial System, and the Economy " MIT Press, Boston (2012). The ultimate goal of this work is to provide reliable financial and monetary measures that can be used by the GCC central banks and the Gulf Monetary Council to improve their database, and hence the monetary policy in the Gulf area. It can also provide financial analysts and economic researchers with access to our statistics.

Table 1-1: Total Foreign Exchange Reserves of GCC Countries (In billions of U.S. dollars)

	2009	%GDP	2010	%GDP	2011	%GDP
Bahrain	3.53	18	4.78	21	4.23	15
Kuwait	17.60	17	18.62	15	22.92	13
Oman	11.85	25	12.67	22	13.98	19
Qatar	17.86	18	30.11	24	15.64	9
Saudi Arabia	396.74	105	432.09	96	525.52	91
UAE	25.07	9	31.75	11	36.09	10

Source: The World Bank.

Table 1-2: The Soundness of the GCC Banking System

Country	Capital Adequacy Ratio		Non-performing Loans (share of gross loans)		Provisioning Rate (% of non-performing loans)	
	2009	2011	2009	2011	2009	2011
Bahrain	19.6	20.3	4.3	4.5	63.9	65.9
Kuwait	16.7	18.5	11.5	7.3	38.3	33.9
Oman	15.5	15.9	2.7	2.4	104	120.6
Qatar	16.1	20.6	1.7	1.7	84.5	86.3
Saudi Arabia	16.5	17.3	3.3	2.3	89.8	132.8
UAE	19.9	21.2	4.3	6.2	94.4	67.8

Source: The International Monetary Fund (IMF), Annual Meeting of Ministers of Finance and Central Bank Governors, Gulf Cooperation Council, Saudi Arabia (2012).

Figure 1-1: Real Gross Domestic Product (Annual Percentage Change)

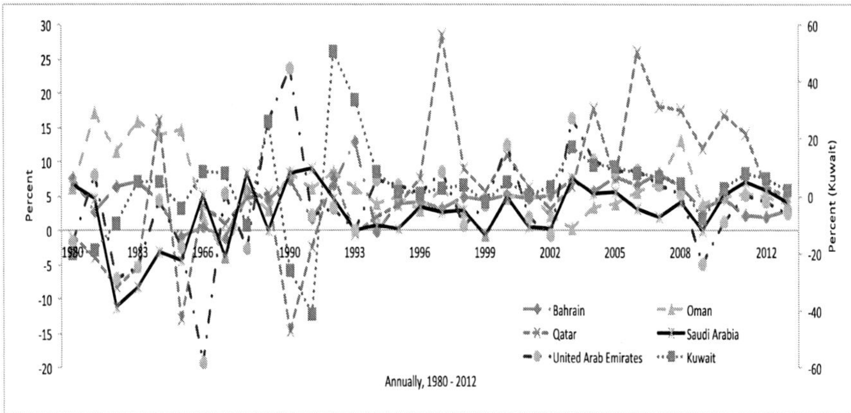

Source: International Financial Statistics (IFS).

Figure 1-2: Annual Inflation Rates

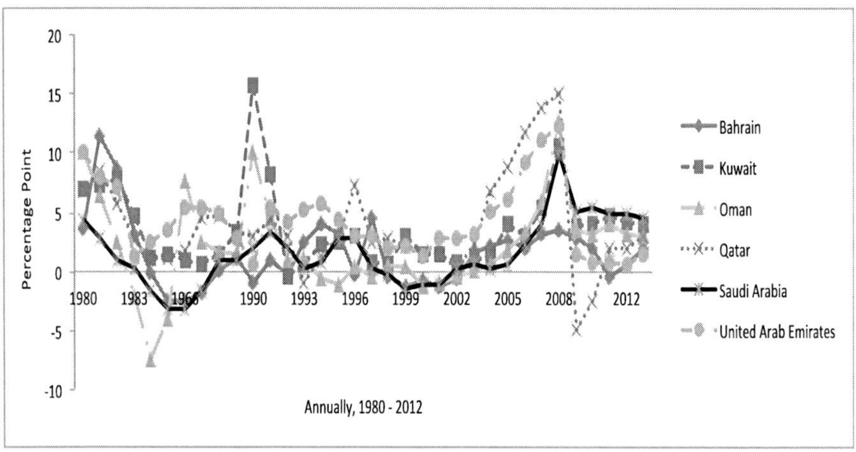

Source: International Financial Statistics (IFS).

Figure 1-3: General Government Balances

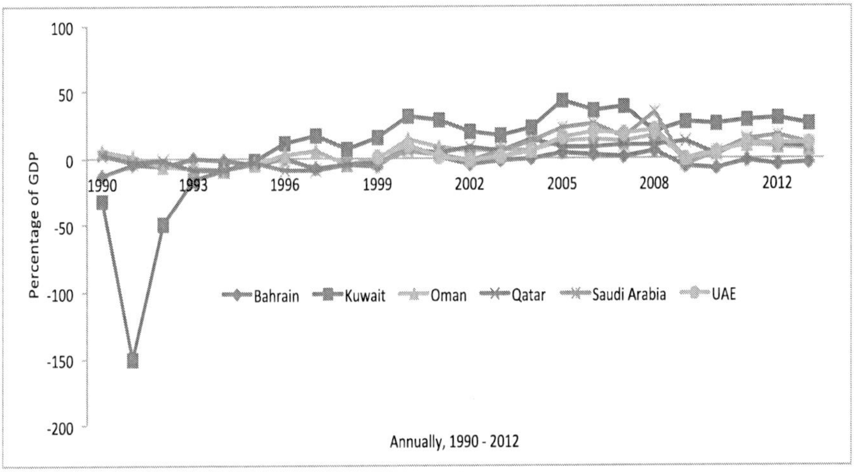

Source: International Financial Statistics (IFS).

CHAPTER TWO

DIVISIA MONETARY AGGREGATES FOR THE GCC COUNTRIES

2.1 Introduction

Monetary authorities and economic agencies worldwide find it challenging yet imperative simultaneously to understand and remedy the recent financial crisis. From the perspective of monetary aggregation and index number theory, the increased frequency and severity of financial crises are imputed in part to the misperceptions among economists, financial analysts, and policy makers about the state of the economy. Particularly, evaluating the economy by means of simple-sum monetary aggregates, having no theoretical foundations whatsoever, can lead to erroneous judgments. Instead, economic decisions must be made based upon solid theoretical foundations, using microeconomic theory and statistical index number theory as proposed by Barnett (1978; 1980a,b; and 1981a). One such index number is the Divisia index.

Barnett (1978; 1980a,b; and 1981a) created Divisia monetary aggregates by linking microeconomic theory with index number theory. The Divisia monetary index is a money supply measure, which weights the monetary components (e.g., currency, demand deposits, and savings and time deposits) according to their usefulness in transactions. The Divisia index accounts for the variability of the share weights among monetary assets within an aggregate, when measuring the monetary service flows of the economy. The index depends upon prices and quantities of monetary assets, where the price of a monetary asset is called its user cost (rental price).

The foundations of the Divisia monetary index are manifested in its solidarity with microeconomics theory. The index also abides by the classification of superlative index numbers defined by Diewert (1976), since the discrete time Divisia index is exact for the quadratic translog specification of the exact aggregator function.[1] Thus, the index is a superlative index endowed with a solid theoretical foundation capable of tracking the exact theoretical monetary aggregate of aggregation theory.[2]

The primary purpose of money is threefold: it is a unit of account, a store of value, and a medium of exchange. A key property of Divisia indexes is their ability to remove the investment motive and measure all other monetary services associated with economic liquidity, by allowing the weights of monetary assets to vary depending on their monetary services at the margin [see Hancock (2005) for a more complete discussion]. The Divisia index, unlike its simple-sum counterpart, accounts for the variability of the share weights among monetary assets within an aggregate, when measuring the monetary service flows of the economy. The investment motive is removed, since otherwise the entire capital stock of the economy would have to be included in the definition of money.

In finance higher returns are often associated with riskier investments, given the rational behavior of investors. Based upon information available at their disposal, investors may choose to invest in low risk assets (e.g., Treasury bills and government bonds) or in riskier assets, such as stocks, options, and other risk-bearing financial instruments. The higher the quality of information and data the investors have, the better qualified they are in making investment decisions. In this regard, Barnett (2012) suggested that inadequate regulations and supervision were not the only factors that caused the subprime financial crisis, but also the low quality of the Federal Reserve published monetary data. Barnett argued that "greed" is an undefined concept in economic theory and instead he points to the defective information provided to the economy by the officially produced simple-sum monetary aggregates, misinforming investors—both individuals and financial institutions—as well as the central bank itself.[3]

The primary pitfall of the simple-sum is its lack of a theoretical foundations. It is a naive index in a sense that it rules out the differences in liquidation and interest-yielding properties of all monetary components (i.e., it implicitly assumes perfect substitutability among monetary assets). The simple-sum index is a special case of the Divisia monetary aggregates under the unrealistic assumption that monetary assets are perfectly

---

[1] Superlative index numbers are exactly correct for a quadratic approximation to the aggregator function. See Barnett (1982) for more details.

[2] Although it is true that the Divisia aggregate exactly tracks the true monetary aggregate in continuous time, the discrete time Törnqvist-Theil approximation tracks the true aggregate to second order accuracy.

[3] See Barnett (2012) for a more complete discussion.

substitutable for one another. However, money currently encompasses monetary assets with different positive rates of returns. As a result, perfect substitutability among assets within an aggregate is no longer a valid assessment. Simple-sum indexes, as pointed out by Barnett (1980b), provide invalid structural economic variables. This assessment advocates for using indexes which measure structural economic variables, as is the subject of index number theory and its associated aggregation theory.

Barnett (1981b, p. 488) comments on the unsatisfactory simple-sum and advocates a formally derivable monetary index:

> "Simple-sum aggregates do not and cannot accurately indicate the quantity of monetary services being provided to the economy. Properly constructed quantity index numbers can. Monetary aggregates should be no less competently constructed than aggregates long available for other economic variables, such as commodity quantities or prices."

The remainder of this chapter is organized as follows: section 2.2 provides a summary of the seminal theoretical considerations relating to the Divisia monetary aggregates; section 2.3 constructs Divisia monetary aggregates for the GCC countries and builds a common Divisia index for the GCC area; section 2.4 discusses the Divisia second moments and the distribution effects; section 2.5 comprises the conclusion.

2.2 The Theory of Divisia Monetary Aggregation

While aggregation and index number theory are highly developed in the fields of consumer demand theory and production theory, they were not applied to monetary theory until Barnett (1978, 1980a,b) derived the correct formula of the price (user cost) of monetary assets and thereby produced a connection between monetary economics and index number theory. User cost is the interest return forgone by holding a monetary asset rather than holding highest return (usually less-liquid) asset. The user cost of money is its opportunity cost and thereby the price of a monetary asset. The seminal work of Barnett (1978; 1980a,b; and 1987) derived the Jorgensonian user cost of monetary assets from a rigorous Fisherine intertemporal consumption expenditure allocation model. His findings have inaugurated the use of index number theory into monetary economics.

The current period nominal user cost of monetary asset i , having quantity m_{it} during period t, is[4]

$$\pi_{it} = p_t^* \frac{R_t - r_{it}}{1+R_t} \tag{2.1}$$

where

R_t is the benchmark rate at time t.
r_{it} is the rate of return on asset i during t.
p_t^* is the true cost-of-living index price at time t.

The user cost nets out the investment motive of holding money, so that the quantity index measures all other serves of the monetary assets. The vector of user-cost prices is $\boldsymbol{\pi}_t$ and the vector of corresponding nominal monetary asset quantities is $\mathbf{m}_t$, while is the vector of real quantities is $\mathbf{m}_t^* = \mathbf{m}_t / p_t^*$.

The Divisia price and quantity indexes solve the following dual differential equations for the price aggregate, $\Pi_t = \Pi(\boldsymbol{\pi}_t)$, and the monetary quantity aggregate, $M_t = M(\mathbf{m}_t)$, respectively:

$$\frac{d\log \Pi_t}{dt} = \sum_i s_{it} \frac{d\log \pi_{it}}{dt} = \sum_i \left(\frac{\pi_{it} m_{it}}{\sum_{k=1}^N \pi_{kt} m_{kt}}\right)\frac{d\log \pi_{it}}{dt} \tag{2.2}$$

$$\frac{d\log M_t}{dt} = \sum_i s_{it} \frac{d\log m_{it}}{dt} = \sum_i \left(\frac{\pi_{it} m_{it}}{\sum_{k=1}^N \pi_{kt} m_{kt}}\right)\frac{d\log m_{it}}{dt} \tag{2.3}$$

where $s_{it} = \dfrac{\pi_{it} m_{it}}{\sum_{k=1}^{N} \pi_{kt} m_{kt}}$ is the expenditure share for the ith monetary asset during period t.

---

[4] The real and nominal user-cost prices are related to one another by the following direct relationship: $\pi_{it} = p_t^* \pi_{it}^*$.

The discrete time representation of the Divisia index is needed for empirical applications, since economic data are measured in discrete time. Törnqvist (1936) and Theil (1967) proved that the Törnqvist-Theil approximation is a second order approximation to the continuous time Divisia index. At time t, the discrete time representation of the Divisia price index, Π_t, over user-cost prices and the Divisia quantity index, M_t, over the monetary components respectively are:[5]

$$log\Pi_t - log\Pi_{t-1} = \sum_{i=1}^{N} s^*_{it}(log\pi_{it} - log\pi_{i,t-1}) \quad (2.4)$$

$$logM_t - logM_{t-1} = \sum_{i=1}^{N} s^*_{it}(logm_{it} - logm_{i,t-1}) \quad (2.5)$$

where $s^*_{it} =$ $(1/2)(s_{it} + s_{i,t-1})$, is the average of the current and lagged expenditure shares s_{it} and $s_{i\ t-1}$.

Equations (2.4) and (2.5) are the weighted averages of the growth rates of user-cost prices, $\boldsymbol{\pi}_t$, and monetary components, $\mathbf{m}_t$, at time t, respectively. In levels, the Divisia monetary index M_t can be written as:

$$\frac{M_t}{M_{t-1}} = \prod_{i=1}^{n}\left(\frac{m_{it}}{m_{i,t-1}}\right)^{s^*_{it}},$$

which is known as the Törnqvist-Theil Divisia monetary quantity index.

Dual to the quantity index, M_t, there is the aggregate price index Π_t, which equals the total expenditue on monetary components divided over the quantity monetary aggregate.[6] More formally,

---

[5] Törnqvist-Theil approximation, which is the Simpson's rule approximation, is commonly used to approximate the Divisia index. See Barnett (1987) for more details.

[6] The quantity index M_t and price index Π_t result from the duality theory under linear homogeneity. Barnett (1987) extended the derivation of the quantity index and price index to the nonhomogeneous case.

$$\Pi_t = \frac{\sum_{i=1}^{N} \pi_{it} m_{it}}{M_t} \tag{2.6}$$

where equation (2.6) satisfies Fisher's factor reversal test:

$$\Pi_t M_t = \sum_{i=1}^{N} \pi_{it} m_{it} \tag{2.7}$$

The Divisia, Paasche, and Laspeyres indexes are not self-dual. As a result, equations (2.4) and (2.6) do not produce exactly the same price aggregate. But the remainder term between them is third order in the changes, and typically less than the roundoff error in the component data.[7]

2.3 Constructing a GCC Area Divisia Monetary Aggregate

A large number of countries maintain Divisia monetary aggregates. While some central banks make these indexes available to the public, many central banks provide and use them only internally. Monetary authorities supplying Divisia monetary aggregates internally or publicly include the Federal Reserve Bank of St. Louis, the European Central Bank, the Bank of England, the Bank of Japan, the Bank of Israel, the National Bank of Poland, and the International Monetary Fund (IMF).[8] While many studies have produced Divisia monetary aggregates data for countries worldwide, there are no Divisia data available for the complete GCC area.[9]

The scarcity of GCC monetary data has limited researchers from exploring and investigating the influence of Divisia aggregation on GCC monetary policy analyses. This paper reports on the first Divisia monetary aggregates for the complete GCC area and focuses on economic

---

[7] See Barnett (1982) for a rigorous discussion on this subject. For nonmathematical explanations, see Barnett (2012).

[8] The Center for Financial Stability (CFS) in New York City provides a directory on the literature pertaining to Divisia monetary aggregations for over 40 countries throughout the world. For more information on Divisia monetary aggregates, visit the CFS website at www.centerforfinancialstability.org/amfm.php.

[9] To date, Alsahafi (2009) is the only paper producing Divisia indexes for a GCC country, and that paper's results are limited to Saudi Arabia.

measurement. Issues related to utility function specifications, parameter estimation, and other econometric applications were avoided.[10] Hence, our reesults are unbiased in the sense that they involve no estimations or inferences at all. We let the data speak for themselves.

Further research can make use of techniques used by the literature on the European Monetary Union (EMU). This literature, highly relevant to the GCC area, includes: Barnett (2003, 2007), Binner, Bissoondeeal, Elger, Gazely, and Mullineux (2005), Binner, Bissoondeeal, Elger, Jones, and Mullineux (2009), Binner, Gazely, and Kendall (2008), Reimers (2002), Stracca (2001), and Beyer, Doornik and Hendry (2000).

Our Divisia monetary indexes for the Gulf States can not only provide the Gulf central banks with a wider range of tools, but also can serve as a vehicle for researchers to improve studies on Gulf monetary policy. Our findings are in line with those of Barnett (2012) and Barnett and Chauvet (2011a,b), in which the discrepancy between Divisia and simple-sum growth rates widened during times of high uncertainty and periods of economic disruptions, such as the financial turmoil. Interestingly, the narrow aggregates were growing while broad aggregates collapsed following the financial crises. This information clearly signals problems with the financial system's ability to create liquidity during the crises.

2.3.1 Data Descriptions and Sources

The six GCC countries—Bahrain, Kuwait, Oman, Qatar, Saudi Arabia, and United Arab Emirates—are the sample countries of this chapter. Variables taken into consideration in the calculation of the Divisia monetary aggregates include: currency in circulation, overnight deposits, demand deposits, savings and time deposits, quasi-money, overnight deposit rates, rate of return on demand deposits, interest rates on savings and time deposits, Treasury bills rates of return, and interest rates on short-term loans. The domestic short-term loan rate is usually the highest and hence used as the benchmark rate for most periods.

The analysis in this study is based on monthly data starting as far as the data were available and ending in December 2011. The GCC central banks are the main sources of monetary data. Interest rates and other monetary data were extracted from the International Financial Statistics (IFS), Federal Reserve Economic Data (FRED), Bloomberg database, and the

[10] Parametric specifications needed for estimating aggregator functions could hinder the objectivity of the data. Index number theory is not dependent upon such specifications. See Barnett (2012) for more details pertaining to monetary aggregation theory and statistical index numbers.

GCC Secretariat General.

All quantities have been seasonally adjusted using the X11 procedure. There were not many missing data in our study. We applied moving average interpolation, whenever data were missing. Conversion from total to per-capita values requires population data, which are only available with annual frequency. To acquire monthly population series, we use linear interpolation.

When used with simple-sum monetary quantity aggregation, the inflation rates for the aggregated Gulf area could be computed as the arithmetic averages of the GCC countries' corresponding inflation rates, to be consistent with the implicit assumption of perfect substitutability embeded in simple-sum quantity aggregation. If willing to make the unreasonable assumption of perfect substitutability among monetary asset quantities, why not be philosophically consistent and make the same unreasonable assumption about consumer goods? But when used with the Divisia monetary quantity indexes, we use Divisia price aggregation over countries.

2.3.2 Benchmark Rate of Return for the GCC Countries

Within the field of aggregation and index number theory, the benchmark rate plays a pivotal role in constructing the Divisia index, since the benchmark rate appears in the user-cost formula for all monetary assets. Barnett (1987) defined the benchmark rate, R_t, to be the yield on a pure investment asset, held solely to accumulate wealth and providing no other services, such as liquidity. The benchmark rate is the interest rate on a theoretical asset held only to transfer wealth over multiperiod planning horizons. During each period, our proxy for the theoretical benchmark rate is the highest rate attained among all relevant assets on which we have data, such as the interest rates on demand deposits, savings and time deposits, loans, government bonds, and Treasury bills. In other words, the benchmark rate, in each period of time, is the maximum rate attained over a set of rates pertaining to monetary assets and other monetary instruments, such as Treasury bills and short-term loans.[11]

In mathematical representation, our benchmark rate takes the following form:

$$R_t = Max\{r_{it}, r_{bills,t}, r_{loan,t}, r_{interbank,t}\}$$

[11] This is called the "envelope approach." See Barnett, Offenbacher, and Spindt (1984) for a complete discussion of this methodology.

where,

r_{it} is the rate of return on asset i during period t.
$r_{bills,t}$ is the interest rate on Treasury bills at time t.
$r_{loan,t}$ is the loan interest rate at time t.
$r_{interbank,t}$ is the interbank interest rate at time t.

2.3.3 Divisia Monetary Aggregates within GCC Countries

Within country Divisia monetary indexes are computed for the GCC countries. We follow the theory provided by Theil (1967) and Barnett (1979a,b; 1980b) and extended in Barnett (2003, 2007) to multilateral aggregation permitting aggregation within and then over countries. The approach uses economic index number theory and assumes the existence of a representative agent within each country. We begin by presenting the theory in continuous time, before converting to discrete time.

Let K be the number of countries in the Gulf Monetary Union. For each country $k \in \{1,...,K\}$, define the true cost-of-living index as $p_k^* = p_k^*(\boldsymbol{p}_k)$, where $\boldsymbol{p}_k = \boldsymbol{p}_k(t)$ represents the vector of prices of consumer goods at time t.[12] Let $\mathbf{x}_k = \mathbf{x}_k(t)$ be the vector of per-capita real rates of consumption of those goods in country k at time t. Let m_{kji} and r_{kji} be, respectively, the nominal per-capita holdings and the yields on asset type i, $i \in \{1, \dots, N\}$, purchased in country j and owned by individual(s) in country k. We enable economic agents within the Gulf area to hold assets in Z outside countries. Moreover, let N_j be the number of different asset types that can be held in country j and let N be the total number of asset types available within all of the relevant countries, $j \in \{1,...,K+Z\}$.[13] Finally, let $R_k = R_k(t)$ and $H_k = H_k(t)$ be the benchmark rate of return and the population of country k at time t, respectively. Hence, the real user-cost price of asset i purchased in country j and owned by economic agent(s) of country k at time t is[14]

---

[12] The theoretical true cost-of-living index is derived from aggregation theory and contains only prices whereas the Consumer Price Index (CPI) formula includes prices and quantities. The CPI is derived from statistical index number theory to approximate the true cost-of-living index nonparametrically [see, e.g., Barnett (2003, 2012) for further discussion].

[13] Clearly $N \geq N_i$ for all $j \in \{1,...,K+Z\}$.

[14] The real and nominal user-cost prices are related to one another as follows: $\pi_{kji}(t) = p_k^*(t)\pi_{kji}^*(t)$.

$$\pi^*_{kji}(t) = R_k(t) - r_{kji}(t)$$

In line with the economic approach proposed by Barnett (1980a,b; 1987), we assume weak separability and linearly homogeneity of the representative agent's utility function u_t.[15] We use the following formal notations:

Let

$$\mathbf{m}^*_{kj} = (m^*_{kj1},\ldots,m^*_{kji},\ldots,m^*_{kjN})'$$

$$\mathbf{m}_{kj} = (m_{kj1},\ldots,m_{kji},\ldots,m_{kjN})'$$

$$\boldsymbol{\pi}^*_{kj} = (\pi^*_{kj1},\ldots,\pi^*_{kji},\ldots,\pi^*_{kjN})'$$

$$\boldsymbol{\pi}_{kj} = (\pi_{kj1},\ldots,\pi_{kji},\ldots,\pi_{kjN})'$$

$$\mathbf{r}_{kj} = (r_{kj1},\ldots,r_{kji},\ldots,r_{kjN})'$$

and let

$$\mathbf{m}^*_{k} = (\mathbf{m}^*_{k1},\ldots,\mathbf{m}^*_{kj},\ldots,\mathbf{m}^*_{k,K+Z})'$$

$$\mathbf{m}_{k} = (\mathbf{m}_{k1},\ldots,\mathbf{m}_{kj},\ldots,\mathbf{m}_{k,K+Z})'$$

$$\boldsymbol{\pi}^*_{k} = (\boldsymbol{\pi}^*_{k1},\ldots,\boldsymbol{\pi}^*_{kj},\ldots,\boldsymbol{\pi}^*_{k,K+Z})'$$

$$\boldsymbol{\pi}_{k} = (\boldsymbol{\pi}_{k1},\ldots,\boldsymbol{\pi}_{kj},\ldots,\boldsymbol{\pi}_{k,K+Z})'$$

$$\mathbf{r}_{k} = (\mathbf{r}_{k1},\ldots,\mathbf{r}_{kj},\ldots,\mathbf{r}_{k,K+Z})'.$$

Our computations are restricted, whenever applicable, to the index set:

$S_k = \{(j,i) : m_{kji} > 0, \quad j \in \{1,\ldots,K+Z\}, i \in \{1,\ldots,N\} \quad \}$ for all $k \in \{1,\ldots,K\}$.

[15] Barnett (1987) incorporated the nonhomothetic case to aggregation and index number theory. Under the nonhomogeneous case, the Divisia index is uniquely considered to be the best element of Diewert's superlative class.

Following Barnett (2003), our Divisia indexes for the Gulf countries can be defined as follows: within each country, $k \in \{1,\ldots,K\}$, the real per-capita monetary services aggregate, M_k^*, the nominal per-capita monetary services aggregate, M_k, the real user-cost price aggregate, Π_k^*, and the nominal user-cost price aggregate, Π_k, respectively are:

$$d\log M_k^* = \sum_{(j,i)\in S_k} w_{kji} d\log m_{kji}^*$$

$$d\log M_k = \sum_{(j,i)\in S_k} w_{kji} d\log m_{kji}$$

$$d\log \Pi_k^* = \sum_{(j,i)\in S_k} w_{kji} d\log \pi_{kji}^*$$

$$d\log \Pi_k = \sum_{(j,i)\in S_k} w_{kji} d\log \pi_{kji}$$

where,

$$w_{kji} = \frac{\pi_{kji} m_{kji}^*}{\boldsymbol{\pi}_k' \mathbf{m}_k^*} = \frac{\pi_{kji}^* m_{kji}^*}{\boldsymbol{\pi}_k^{*\prime} \mathbf{m}_k^*} = \frac{(R_k - r_{kji}) m_{kji}^*}{\sum_{(j,i)\in S_k} (R_k - r_{kji}) m_{kji}^*} = \frac{(R_k - r_{kji}) m_{kji}}{\sum_{(j,i)\in S_k} (R_k - r_{kji}) m_{kji}}.$$

Notice that $0 \le w_{kji} \le 1$ for all $k \in \{1,\ldots,K\}$, $j \in \{1,\ldots,K+Z\}$, and $i \in \{1,\ldots,N\}$. Moreover, $\sum_{(j,i)\in S_k} w_{kji} = 1$ for all $k \in \{1,\ldots,K\}$ implies that the shares, w_{kji}, possess the properties of a probability distribution for each country $k \in \{1,\ldots,K\}$. Consequently, the above Divisia indexes could be interpreted as Divisia growth rate means.[16]

The equivalent discrete time representation of the above continues time Divisia indexes are, respectively:

[16] This is a statistical representation of the Divisia growth rate means. See Barnett (2003) for an alternative representation.

$$\log M_{kt}^* - \log M_{k,t-1}^* = \sum_{(j,i)\in S_k} w_{kjit}^* (\log m_{kjit}^* - \log m_{kji,t-1}^*)$$

$$\log M_{kt} - \log M_{k,t-1} = \sum_{(j,i)\in S_k} w_{kjit}^* (\log m_{kjit} - \log m_{kji,t-1})$$

$$\log \Pi_{kt}^* - \log \Pi_{k,t-1}^* = \sum_{(j,i)\in S_k} w_{kjit}^* (\log \pi_{kjit}^* - \log \pi_{kji,t-1}^*)$$

$$\log \Pi_{kt} - \log \Pi_{k,t-1} = \sum_{(j,i)\in S_k} w_{kjit}^* (\log \pi_{kjit} - \log \pi_{kji,t-1}),$$

where $w_{kjit}^* = (1/2)\left(w_{kjit} + w_{kji,t-1}\right)$.

In levels, the real and nominal per-capita Divisia monetary indexes, respectively, are

$$\frac{M_{kt}^*}{M_{k,t-1}^*} = \prod_{(j,i)\in S_k} \left(\frac{m_{kjit}^*}{m_{kji,t-1}^*}\right)^{w_{kjit}^*}$$

and

$$\frac{M_{kt}}{M_{k,t-1}} = \prod_{(j,i)\in S_k} \left(\frac{m_{kjit}}{m_{kji,t-1}}\right)^{w_{kjit}^*}.$$

By Fisher's factor reversal test, there exists a user-cost price aggregate dual to the exact service quantity aggregate such that their product equals the total expenditure on the components. More formally,

$$\Pi_{kt} M_{kt} = \sum_{(j,i)\in S_k} \pi_{kjit} m_{kjit},$$

The exact user-cost aggregate price dual to the exact quantity aggregate is thereby obtained by dividing actual expenditure on the components by the quantity aggregate, as follows:

$$\Pi_{kt} = \frac{\sum_{(j,i)\in S_k} \pi_{kjit} m_{kjit}}{M_{kt}}.$$

The literature on interest rate aggregation is different from the literature relevant to economic aggregation and index-number theory. Unlike user-cost aggregation, which is a form of price aggregation, interest rate aggregation is based on elementary accounting principles. Let $\tilde{R}_{kt}$ be country k's aggregate interest rate at time t. A portfolio of monetary assets $\{\boldsymbol{m}_{kt} : (j,i) \in S_k\}$ with interest rates $\{\boldsymbol{r}_{kt} : (j,i) \in S_k\}$ has investment yield $\sum_{(j,i)\in S_k} r_{kjit} m_{kjit}$. Hence, the following accounting identity must hold, in order for $\tilde{R}_{kt}$ to be the rate of return on the portfolio:

$$\tilde{R}_{kt} \sum_{(j,i)\in S_k} m_{kjit} = \sum_{(j,i)\in S_k} r_{kjit} m_{kjit}.$$

Solving for $\tilde{R}_{kt}$, we acquire

$$\tilde{R}_{kt} = \frac{\sum_{(j,i)\in S_k} r_{kjit} m_{kjit}}{\sum_{(j,i)\in S_k} m_{kjit}}.$$

This paper defines Divisia monetary aggregates in GCC countries as following: the narrowed Divisia monetary aggregate, D1, will contain both currency in circulation and demand deposits. As in M2, the broader Divisia monetary aggregate, D2, will include D1 plus savings and time deposits. The central bank of Qatar, in turn, incorporates quasi-money within the broader monetary aggregates. Consequently, the Divisia monetary aggregates will be slightly different for Qatar relative to the others.[17]

Figure 2-1 contains plots of the year-over-year growth rates of the narrow Divisia and simple-sum monetary aggregates for the GCC countries. The two approaches to aggregation produce identical results, since all assets within the monetary aggregates bear zero-interest rates and

[17] The inclusion of the quasi–money in the broader monetary aggregate is based solely on data availability.

therefore have the same user-cost prices.[18] Specifically, currency in circulation and demand deposits are zero-interest assets, and hence the theory implies that consumers are indifferent between those two assets.[19]

By construction, broad monetary aggregates contain assets with positive interest rates. Assuming perfect substitutability among assets yielding different interest rates is not permissible.[20] For most countries (and the GCC as a whole) the imperfect substitutability among those assets leads to distinct results between Divisia and simple-sum aggregates —suggesting that policy makers may reach different conclusions based on the different aggregation procedures.

Figure 2-2 displays the year-over-year growth rates of the broad Divisia and simple-sum monetary aggregates for the GCC countries. The most interesting charts are reported for Kuwait and Saudi Arabia, where the year-over-year growth rates for the broad Divisia and simple-sum aggregates interchangeably shift over time. For instance, in Kuwait there has been a rotation between the year-over-year growth rates of the broad Divisia and simple-sum. Divisia growth rates fluctuate from being above simple-sum during mid 2000 to mid 2004 and to being below from early 2006 to late 2007. The broad Divisia growth rates diverge from simple-sum as a result of the high variation in the user costs of the monetary components. This variation suggests that monetary assets in Kuwait are less substitutable. The Divisia indexes fall sharply as the demand deposits (called sight deposits) in Kuwait spiked in mid-1995 from being 823.4 million in May up to 1081.5 and then fell back to 810.3 in July. Divisia indexes were able to signal such economic disruptions in the monetary system.

The Saudi capital market plunged in 2006. Specifically, the Saudi stock market meltdown in 2006 was accurately captured by the Divisia monetary indexes, in which the year-over-year growth rates for Divisia fell sharply during the first six months of 2006 to almost zero percent and

---

[18] The interest rates on demand deposits in Qatar offer positive interest rates. Since demand deposits' interest rates are low, while the benchmark rates are exceptionally high, the user–cost prices of currency in circulation and demand deposits are relatively similar.

[19] Some papers impute an implicit rate of return on demand deposits [see, e.g., Klein (1974) and Startz (1979)]. Alsahafi (2009) constructed Divisia monetary index for Saudi Arabia with an implicit rate of return imputed to demand deposits. Nevertheless, given the fact that there is neither public data nor solid evidence on such an imputation, we exclude implied interest rates on demand deposits.

[20] Perfect substitutability among assets exists, if and only if, all assets within an aggregate offer the same rate of return.

bounced up to reach their maximum in early 2008 (Figure 2-2).[21] During the recent financial crisis, the Divisia growth rate fluctuated from being above simple-sum in late 2008 to being below in early 2009. This result indicates that the monetary policy was more contractionary than likely intended during the financial crisis, when the Divisia monetary aggregates growth rates were lower than their simple-sum counterparts.

In 1998, when the price of oil dropped and reached minimum levels (approximately $10 per barrel) for more than two decades, thereby adversely affecting the domestic economy, the Omani monetary policy endeavored to stabilize the economy.[22] This led to a one-year hiatus between the year-over-year growth rates of Divisia and simple-sum indexes (Figure 2-2).

In Bahrain, steady growth prevailed from 2000 to 2005, but the year-over-year monetary growth accelerated afterwards to attain its peak in early 2008, in response to the boom of oil prices (Figure 2-2). However, the growth fell sharply in mid-2008, as a result of the sudden drop of energy prices. The recently erupted demonstrations and civil uprisings, called the "Arab Spring" , during which the Bahraini government has declared a three-month state of emergency, have hindered economic reintegration.

In Qatar, the growth rates of the narrow monetary aggregate are fairly stable except in late 2008 when demand for deposits witnessed a transitory decline (more than 20%). The year-over-year growth rates reveal a downward trend from mid-2008 to 2009, during which the Qatari central bank aimed to subdue staggering inflation (Figure 2-1). Similarly, the growth rates for the broader aggregates illustrate the central banks effort in deflating the economy as plotted in Figure 2-2.

The openness of the UAE economy has made the country more vulnerable to the financial crisis. During the crisis, Abu Dhabi Investment Authority (one of the world's larger investment funds) declared losses of $125 billion. Moreover, Dubai was bailed out after the property bust degraded the country's economic position.[23] In addition to these factors,

---

[21] The spike of the Divisia growth rate was likely driven by high oil prices in early to mid-2008.

[22] Oman is not a member of the Organization of the Petroleum Exporting Countries (OPEC). Nevertheless, oil and other petroleum products continue to play a significant role in shaping the economy. For more information about the oil industry, see the statistical bulletins reported by the Omani Ministry of Oil and Gas.

[23] Dubai has received a $10 billion bail-out mostly from its neighbor state Abu Dhabi to enable Dubai to pay off the immediate debts of its most troubled state-run companies.

high inflation rates (above 12%) have further imposed economic challenges upon the UAE monetary authorities. The most notable difference between Divisia and simple-sum indexes took place during 2006-2007 and 2009-2010. Those periods include the toughest economic challenges the UAE has faced (Figure 2-2). However, the year-over-year growth rates for both indexes dropped sharply from 50% in 2008 to around 5% in 2009. The rise in the monetary aggregates corresponds to the boom in oil prices during early 2008. Meanwhile, the following collapse of the aggregates' growth rates corresponds with the financial crises, which lowered global demand for oil, driving down the prices.

The behavioral patterns of the user-cost prices, aggregate interest rates, dual prices, and growth rates of the Divisia aggregate user-cost prices could be used as an "economic stability" indicator. User-cost prices often tend to go in different directions during periods of higher economic uncertainty [see Barnett, Fisher, and Serletis (1992)]. Our data seem to support this claim. Plots of the user-cost prices reveal that the user-cost prices of non-liquid monetary assets (e.g., savings and time deposits, and quasi-money) tend to be more volatile and unstable during financial crises as opposed to milder economic periods (Figure 2-3). Moreover, the dual prices and growth rates of the broader Divisia user-cost aggregates are more volatile during times of economic uncertainty (Figures 2-4 and 2-5). The aggregate interest rate of the narrow monetary aggregate, M1, is equal to zero for all GCC countries, except for Qatar, in which demand deposits yield positive interest rates. The aggregate interest rates corresponding to the broader monetary aggregate, M2, fluctuated the most during the recent financial crisis (Figure 2-6). In 2011, aggregate interest rates remained below one percentage point as the GCC central banks set expansionary monetary policy to mitigate the effects of the recent financial crisis on Gulf economies.

2.3.4 Divisia Monetary Aggregates over GCC Countries: A Heterogeneous Agents Approach

There has been a recurring tendency toward higher economic integration among Gulf countries. Fueled by the increasing multilateral trade in the region, the Gulf Cooperation Council (GCC) has proposed its sentiment about launching a single monetary union, where indivisible monetary policies will be implemented simultaneously for all member states. Hence, the Gulf Monetary Council (GMC) was established in March 2010. Oman and UAE have opted out of the GMC for different reasons. In 2006, Oman withdrew from the monetary union, for which it has not met the convergence criteria required for joining the GMC. In 2009, UAE had a dispute over the location of the GMC being headquartered in Riyadh, the capital of Saudi Arabia.[24] While negotiations are still ongoing, these factors have hindered the debut of the common currency for the Gulf area. In addition to these factors, the growing uncertainty about the world economy, and specifically the intensifying fears of the European sovereign debt crisis, have led the GMC to postpone its commencement of a common currency towards 2015.

Upon the completion of the common monetary policy in the Euro area, a large number of the studies in the monetary aggregation literature have used the following two approaches for measuring monetary service flows aggregated over the euro-zone: (i) the direct approach and (ii) the indirect approach. The former approach aggregates assets of a specific type over all countries by simply adding them up and then using the techniques provided by the Divisia index to obtain the overall monetary aggregate. The latter approach constructs Divisia aggregates across countries but uses *ad hoc* weighted averages (e.g., GDP weights) for the over-countries' aggregates. Barnett (2003) explained the drawbacks of these approaches: the direct approach requires very restrictive assumptions, whereas the indirect approach violates aggregation theory and does not produce nesting of the multilateral or unilateral representative agent approaches. Using *ad hoc* weighted averages of inflation rates over countries to produce a single inflation rate for the euro area is unsatisfactory and inconsistent with index number theory.

Barnett (1982) describes the phases that lead into optimal monetary aggregation in the following manner:

> **Stage 1:** carefully determine the sets of monetary assets, such that the assets to be consolidated within an aggregate pass a separability test validating the grouping. This criterion implies that the sets of monetary assets are well-defined, based upon the statistical properties as well as the monetary services pertaining to these assets.[25]
>
> **Stage 2:** construct an index number formula from the superlative index number class for each admissible set of monetary assets acquired in stage

[24] The UAE has demanded to be the host country for the GMC, since it has the second largest economy in the GCC area, after Saudi Arabia.

[25] Weak separability of the utility function is assumed in this paper. Many empirical studies provide tests for weak separability. See, for example, Barnett and de Peretti (2009), Barnett and Choi (1989), Blackorby, Russell, and Primont (1998), de Peretti (2005, 2007), Fleissig and Whitney (2003, 2005), Swofford and Whitney (1987, 1994), and Varian (1982, 1983, and 1985). To our knowledge, Barnett and de Peretti (2009) offer the most promising test.

1. The Divisia index is not the only obtainable superlative index, but all index numbers in that class move closely together.[26]

Stage 3: examine the interaction among the relevant macro-economic variables and the index numbers. This assessment can be carried out by means of empirical studies. The findings will determine optimal monetary aggregation.

Three increasingly restrictive approaches were developed by Barnett (2003, 2007) to capture the economic convergence dynamics evolving in the Euro zone. These approaches, starting from least restrictive approach, are: the heterogeneous agents approach, the multilateral representative agent approach, and the unilateral representative agent approach. The European Central Bank has benefited the most from this research in enhancing its Divisia monetary aggregates database provided to the ECB's Governing Council at its meetings.

In the following section, the Divisia monetary indexes are constructed over the GCC area. The findings suggest that while narrow monetary indexes are closely alike, the broad Divisia index outperforms its simple-sum counterpart. For the growth rates of the Divisia and simple-sum monetary aggregates over the GCC countries, Divisia growth rates display business cycle patterns that are consistent with monetary policy.

A large portion of the present paper is based upon the seminal work done by Barnett (1979a;1979b;1980a,b), developed further by Barnett (2003, 2007). In line with the heterogeneous agents approach proposed by Barnett (2003, 2007), we assume the existence of a representative consumer within countries in the Gulf union and treat the union's representative consumers as heterogeneous agents. This introduces us to a heterogeneous countries approach to aggregation over countries. Let K be the number of countries in the Gulf monetary union.

In continuous time, let

$s_k(t) = H_k(t)/\sum_{k=1}^{K} H_k(t)$ be country $k's$ share of total GCC area population at time t.[27]

$I_k = I_k(t)$ be country $k's$ total expenditure at time t.

---

[26] Fisher (1922) considered eleven superlative index numbers, including the Divisia index.

[27] s_k is used to convert to per–capita values and we basically drop it to obtain total values.

e_{kt} be country $k's$ currency exchange rate against a market basket of currencies at t.

$X_k = g_k(x_k)$ be country $k's$ consumer-goods per-capita quantity aggregate over $\mathbf{x}_k$.

Consider a representative agent h who lives in country $k \in \{1,...,K\}$ with the utility function:

$$U_h = U_h[u_h(\mathbf{m}_h^*), g_h(\mathbf{x}_h)] = U[u(\mathbf{m}_h^*, \phi_h), g(\mathbf{x}_h, \phi_h), \phi_h]$$

for all tastes , ϕ_h, in the Gulf area.[28] While U, u, and g are fixed functions, the corresponding functions U_h, u_h, and g_h are random functions.[29] Furthermore, assume that the representative agent, h, within country $k \in \{1,..., K\}$ solves the following maximization problem for $(\mathbf{m}_h^*, \mathbf{x}_h)$ during period t:[30]

$$\text{maximize } U[u(\mathbf{m}_h^*, \phi_h), g(\mathbf{x}_h, \phi_h), \phi_h]$$
$$\text{subject to}$$
$$\mathbf{m}_h^{*'}\boldsymbol{\pi}_h + \mathbf{x}_h'\mathbf{p}_h = I_h.$$

Define

$$W_k = \frac{M_k^* \Pi_k^* p_k^* s_k e_k}{\sum_{k=1}^K M_k^* \Pi_k^* p_k^* s_k e_k} = \frac{M_k \Pi_k^* s_k e_k}{\sum_{k=1}^K M_k \Pi_k^* s_k e_k} = \frac{M_k^* \Pi_k s_k e_k}{\sum_{k=1}^K M_k^* \Pi_k s_k e_k}$$

to be the kth country's expenditure share of the Gulf union's monetary service flow at time t. Similar to the share weight for single country,

---

28 The second equality is an immediate result of the assumption that differences in tastes across countries can be explained via a vector of taste–determining variables, ϕ_h. See Barnett (2003) for more details.

29 Barnett (2003, 2007) rigorously explained the properties of these functions and their nested variables.

30 See Barnett (2003, 2007) for additional assumptions for the joint distribution of the random variables $(I_h, \mathbf{p}_h, e_h, \boldsymbol{\pi}_h, \phi_h)$ to exist.

notice that $0 \le W_k \le 1$ and $\sum_{k=1}^{K} W_k = 1$ are satisfied for the union's expenditure shares, so that we can treat $\{W_1, \ldots, W_K\}$ as a probability distribution for our Divisia indexes.

The Gulf area's nominal per-capita monetary services flow, M, real per-capita monetary services flow, M^*, nominal monetary user-cost price, Π, real monetary user-cost price, Π^*, and the Gulf area's Divisia Consumer Price Indexes, $p^* = p^*(t)$, and $P^* = P^*(t)$, are defined as follows, where there are two alternative ways of weighting inflation across countries:[31]

$$\frac{d \log M}{dt} = \sum_{k=1}^{K} W_k \frac{d \log(M_k s_k e_k)}{dt}$$

$$\frac{d \log M^*}{dt} = \sum_{k=1}^{K} W_k \frac{d \log(M_k^* s_k)}{dt}$$

$$\frac{d \log \Pi}{dt} = \sum_{k=1}^{K} W_k \frac{d \log(\Pi_k e_k)}{dt}$$

$$\frac{d \log \Pi^*}{dt} = \sum_{k=1}^{K} W_k \frac{d \log(\Pi_k^*)}{dt}$$

$$\frac{d \log P^*}{dt} = \sum_{k=1}^{K} B_k \frac{d \log(p_k^* e_k)}{dt}$$

$$\frac{d \log p^*}{dt} = \sum_{k=1}^{K} W_k \frac{d \log(p_k^* e_k)}{dt}$$

where country k's expenditure share of Gulf consumption is

---

[31] Barnett (2003) proved the relationship between the nominal versus real variables hold, so that $\Pi = \Pi^* p^*$ and $M = M^* p^*$.

$$B_k = \frac{X_k p_k^* e_k}{\sum_{k=1}^{K} X_k p_k^* e_k}$$

The corresponding discrete time Divisia growth indexes for the GCC monetary union are:

$$\log M_t - \log M_{t\text{-}1} = \sum_{k=1}^{K} W_{kt}^* (\log M_{kt}\, s_{kt}\, e_{kt} - \log M_{k,t\text{-}1}\, s_{k,t\text{-}1}\, e_{k,t\text{-}1})$$

$$\log M_t^* - \log M_{t-1}^* = \sum_{k=1}^{K} W_{kt}^* (\log M_{kt}^*\ s_{kt} - \log M_{k,t-1}^* s_{k,t\text{-}1})$$

$$\log \Pi_t - \log \Pi_{t\text{-}1} = \sum_{k=1}^{K} W_{kt}^* (\log \Pi_{kt}\, e_{kt} - \log \Pi_{k,t\text{-}1}\, e_{k,t\text{-}1})$$

$$\log \Pi_t^* - \log \Pi_{t-1}^* = \sum_{k=1}^{K} W_{kt}^* (\log \Pi_{kt}^* - \log \Pi_{k,t-1}^*)$$

$$\log P_t^* - \log P_{t-1}^* = \sum_{k=1}^{K} B_{kt}^* (\log p_{kt}^*\ e_{kt} - \log p_{k,t-1}^*\ e_{k,t\text{-}1})$$

$$\log p_t^* - \log p_{t-1}^* = \sum_{k=1}^{K} W_{kt}^* (\log p_{kt}^*\ e_{kt} - \log p_{k,t-1}^*\ e_{k,t\text{-}1})$$

where $W_{kt}^* = (1/2)(W_{kt} + W_{k,t-1})$ and $B_{kt}^* = (1/2)(B_{kt} + B_{k,t-1})$.

In levels, the nominal and real per-capita Divisia monetary indexes, respectively, are

$$\frac{M_t}{M_{t-1}} = \prod_{k=1}^{K} \left(\frac{M_{kt} s_{kt} e_{kt}}{M_{k,t-1} s_{k,t-1} e_{k,t-1}}\right)^{W_{kt}^*}$$

and

$$\frac{M_t^*}{M_{t-1}^*} = \prod_{k=1}^{K} \left(\frac{M_{kt}^* s_{kt}}{M_{k,t-1}^* s_{k,t-1}}\right)^{W_{kt}^*}$$

Observe that Fisher's factor reversal property holds for the monetary quantity and user-cost aggregates over countries. The total expenditure on monetary services aggregated over countries would be the same, whether obtained by multiplying the monetary union's quantity by its user-cost aggregates or by the sum of the products within countries [see Barnett (2003) for a complete proof]. This result leads to Fisher's factor reversal test for the Gulf area:

$$M_t^* \Pi_t = \sum_{k=1}^{K} (M_{kt}^* \Pi_{kt} s_{kt} e_{kt}).$$

Given the above relation, the price dual to the Gulf area Divisia monetary aggregates could be easily computed by dividing expendure by the Gulf monetary aggregate, M^*, so that

$$\Pi_t = \frac{\sum_{k=1}^{K} (M_{kt}^* \Pi_{kt} s_{kt} e_{kt})}{M_t^*}$$

Analogously to the within country case, the aggregate interest rate for the GCC monetary union is:

$$\tilde{R}_t = \frac{\sum_{k=1}^{K} (\sum_{(j,i) \in S_k} m_{kjit}) \tilde{R}_{kt} e_{kt}}{\sum_{k=1}^{K} (\sum_{(j,i) \in S_k} m_{kjit}) e_{kt}} = \frac{\sum_{k=1}^{K} (\sum_{(j,i) \in S_k} r_{kjit} m_{kjit}) e_{kt}}{\sum_{k=1}^{K} (\sum_{(j,i) \in S_k} m_{kjit}) e_{kt}}.$$

Figures 2-1 and 2-2 depict the year-over-year growth rates of the Divisia and simple-sum aggregated over the GCC countries. The narrow monetary Divisia growth rates for the GCC union are equivalent to their counterpart simple-sum indexes—as is the case for each single country (Figure 2-1). The Divisia growth rates of the broad monetary aggregates differ from the simple-sums (Figure 2-2). The year-over-year Divisia growth rates remarkably exemplify the business cycles, during which the growth rates are high in the economic boom—fueled by large oil revenues and massive government spending on infrastructure projects—and low afterwards, in periods when oil prices dropped sharply as a consequence of the distress over the global economy. Figure 2-2 shows that the hump-shaped Divisia year-over-year growth rates are more evident than the simple-sum's. Specifically, Divisia year-over-year growth rates have outreached the simple-sum's. Divisia growth was below simple sum's during recessions, while above throughout expansionary phases. The findings suggest that the Gulf monetary council, if guided by the simple sum, may overreact by implementing an excessive contractionary/expansionary policy, when it is not needed.

Figure 2-7 depicts the annual Divisia inflation rate versus the arithmetic average inflation rate. At the beginning of the recent financial crises, the Divisia inflation rate diverged from its counterpart and remained relatively higher than the arithmetic average inflation rate. Since the inflation rate would be underestimated under the arithmetic average inflation rate, the GMC monetary policy would be based upon misleading data, if the GMC were to use the arithmetic average price index, as would be philosophically consistent with the simple-sum approach to aggregation over imperfect substitutes.

The user-cost prices, aggregate interest rates, and growth rates of the Divisia aggregate user-cost prices may serve as economic stability indicator for the GCC area. A high (low) variation of these growths over time is associated with high (low) economic uncertainty. Figures 2-4, 2-5, and 2-6 indicate that the aggregate interest rates, dual prices, and the growth rates of Divisia aggregate user-cost prices of the broader Divisia aggregates for the GCC area are more volatile than the narrow aggregtes during the recent financial crises. The findings suggest a high correlation between the broad monetary aggregates and the world economy. Moreover, Divisia monetary aggregates provide critical information about inside liquidity created by financial intermediaries. In the aftermath of financial crises, the narrow aggregates were growing, while simultaneously the broad aggregates plunged, indicating the shortfall of financial intermediaries in creating inside money (Figures 2-1 and 2-2).

2.4 Divisia Second Moments and the Distribution Effects

We have seen the major role of Divisia growth means in constructing the Divisia monetary aggregates. We extend our analyses further to the Divisia second moments. Divisia variances measure the degree to which monetary policy affects countries differently within a union. Exploiting the Divisia second moments is of particular importance, especially to the GMC [see Barnett (2003)]. Our GCC Divisia variances capture the distribution effects within Gulf countries and simultaneously measure the progress made towards monetary and financial convergence. Providing the Divisia second moments can not only help to identify the distribution effects of the single monetary policy, but can also supply the GMC with additional tools to gauge the dynamics of monetary policy.[32]

As above, define country k's expenditure share of the Gulf consumption by:

$$B_k = \frac{X_k p_k^* e_k}{\sum_{k=1}^{K} X_k p_k^* e_k}$$

and define

$$d\log W = \sum_{k=1}^{K} W_k d\log W_k$$

The Divisia growth rate variances computed about their means, across the Gulf countries, are defined as:

[32] By connecting user–cost and monetary service growth rates, Barnett (2003) provided an additional measure of the effectiveness of transmission mechanisms that operate through interest rates. Since the GMC monetary policy is committed to the de facto pegging of its exchange rate to the US dollar, rather than operating through interest rates, we preclude interest rate indicators from our study.

$$\Omega = \sum_{k=1}^{K} W_k [d\log(M_k s_k e_k) - d\log M]^2$$

$$\Omega^* = \sum_{k=1}^{K} W_k [d\log(M^*{}_k s_k) - d\log M^*]^2$$

$$\Phi = \sum_{k=1}^{K} W_k [d\log(\Pi_k e_k) - d\log \Pi]^2$$

$$\Phi^* = \sum_{k=1}^{K} W_k [d\log(\Pi_k^*) - d\log \Pi^*]^2$$

$$\Psi = \sum_{k=1}^{K} W_k [d\log(W_k) - d\log W]^2$$

$$\Gamma_M = \sum_{k=1}^{K} W_k [d\log(p_k^* e_k) - d\log p^*]^2$$

$$\Gamma = \sum_{k=1}^{K} B_k [d\log(p_k^* e_k) - d\log P^*]^2$$

where Ω and Ω^* are the Divisia monetary services growth rate variances in nominal and real terms, respectively. Similarly, Φ and Φ^* are the Divisia aggregate user-cost growth rate variances, while Ψ is the growth rate variance of the Divisia monetary services expenditure-share. Lastly, Γ_M and Γ denote the Divisia inflation variances, with the alternative weighting methods, one based on consumption sector weighting and the other based on monetary sector weighting. The indexes Ω and Ω^* are measures of the dispersion of monetary growth rates across GCC countries in nominal terms, whereas Ψ is the measure in real terms. Moreover, Γ and Γ_M are measures of the dispersion of the GCC inflation rates.[33] The Divisia aggregate user-cost growth rate variances, Φ and Φ^*, indicate the progress of synchronization in the financial markets of the GCC countries. The values of Ω, Ω^*, Ψ, Γ_M, and Γ measure the distribution effects of the

[33] See Barnett (2003, 2007) for more details.

GMC monetary policy over the GCC area. Interestingly, decreasing values of Ω, Ω^*, Ψ, and Γ indicators of economic harmonization among GCC countries and more uniform effects of monetary policy over the GCC countries. These indicators can be used not only to monitor the progress of harmonization over the GCC economies, but also to serve as a measure of the monetary policy's effects across the Gulf area.

Excluding the effects of the recent financial crisis, the variances of the monetary services and expenditure share growth rates of the GCC area suggest that the GCC countries have been highly synchronized (Figures 2-8 and 2-9). Figure 2-10 shows that the Divisia aggregate user-cost growth rate variances have been consistently low, with the exception of 2008 and 2009. More importantly, the growth rate variances, Φ, of the Divisia aggregate user cost have remained close to zero, implying that the financial markets have become even more synchronized recently. The Divisia inflation rate variances fluctuate over time from being high during periods of economic unrest to being low in times of economic prosperity (Figure 2-11). The high variances are, respectively, associated with periods of meltdown of the Saudi stock markets, global financial crises, and Arab Spring uprisings in Bahrain.

2.5 Conclusion

It is a well-known fact that the broader the monetary aggregate, the more obvious the deficiency of the simple-sum index in measuring the amount of monetary services injected into the economy. The implicit assumption made when using simple-sum monetary aggregates is that all components are perfect one-for-one substitutes in producing liquidity services. Broad aggregates, which group currency with government bonds, will certainly fail to satisfy this assumption. At broad levels of aggregation, simple-sum measures can be very misleading and diverge from the properly weighted Divisia aggregates.

The major drawback of the officially published simple-sum monetary aggregates is its lack of theoretical foundations. For monetary policy to be more effective, the policymaker's decisions should be based upon data with valid economic meaning (i.e., computed by techniques developed in the fields of aggregation and index number theory). A key property of the Divisia index lies in its compatibility with microeconomic aggregation theory.

In 1980, Barnett originated the Divisia monetary aggregates for the United States. The number of central banks and financial organizations employing the Divisia indexes has been growing since then. Building the

Divisia monetary indexes for the Gulf area can facilitate transforming the GCC central banks to be among the leading central banks maintaining Divisia monetary aggregates.

Using the heterogeneous agents approach to aggregation over countries, based on Theil (1967) and Barnett (1979a,b; 1980a,b) and developed further in Barnett (2003, 2007), we construct the Divisia monetary index for the GCC area. Our findings confirm the dominance of the Divisia indexes in displaying a business cycle pattern that is consistent with GCC monetary policy. Specifically, Divisia monetary growth rates are low prior to recessions, while those growth rates increase at a faster pace than simple-sum during recoveries.

Moreover, we explore the distribution effects of policy within the GCC monetary union and examine the progress towards economic convergence by utilizing Divisia second moments. The results indicate that monetary policy for GCC countries are highly synchronized. Hence a common GCC monetary policy will have a uniform effect over member countries. In addition, there is direct evidence of progress towards harmonization of financial markets over GCC countries.

We propose an economic stability indicator for the GCC area, by analyzing the dynamics pertaining to certain variables such as the dual price aggregate, aggregate interest rates, and the growth rates of Divisia aggregate user-cost. High variation of these variables over time is a sign of high economic uncertainty and vice versa. Our indicator performs well in detecting periods of economic distress, namely the recent financial crises.

References

Alsahafi, M. (2009). Linear and non-linear techniques for estimating the money demand function: The case of Saudi Arabia. *3378928,* University of Kansas.

Barnett, W. A. (1978). The user cost of money. *Economics Letters, 1*(2), 145-149.

—. (1979a). The Joint Allocation of Leisure and Goods Expenditure. *Econometrica, 47*(3), 539-563.

—. (1979b). Theoretical Foundations for the Rotterdam Model. *Review of Economic Studies, 46*(1), 109-130.

—. (1980a). Economic monetary aggregates--reply. *Journal of Econometrics, 14*(1), 57-59.

—. (1980b). Economic monetary aggregates an application of index number and aggregation theory. *Journal of Econometrics, 14*(1), 11-48.

—. (1981a). Consumer demand and labor supply: goods, monetary assets, and time. *Elsevier, Amsterdam.*
—. (1981b). The New Monetary Aggregates: A Comment. *Journal of Money, Credit and Banking, 13*(4), 485-489.
—. (1982). The Optimal Level of Monetary Aggregation. *Journal of Money, Credit and Banking, 14*(4), 687-710.
—. (1987). The Microeconomic Theory of Monetary Aggregation. *New Approaches to Monetary Economics,* Cambridge U. Press.
—. (2003). Aggregation-Theoretic Monetary Aggregation over the Euro Area, when Countries are Heterogeneous. *EconWPA.*
—. (2007). Multilateral aggregation-theoretic monetary aggregation over heterogeneous countries. *Journal of Econometrics, 136*(2), 457-482.
—. (2012). Getting it wrong : how faulty monetary statistics undermine the Fed, the financial system, and the economy. MIT Press, Boston.
Barnett, W. A., and Chauvet, M. (2011a). How better monetary statistics could have signaled the financial crisis. *Journal of Econometrics, 161*(1), 6-23.
Barnett, W. A., and Chauvet, M. (2011b). Financial Aggregation and Index Number Theory. *World Scientific Books. (Vol.2): World Scientific Publishing Co. Pte. Ltd.*
Barnett, W. A., and Choi, S. (1989). A Monte Carlo Study of Tests of Blockwise Weak Separability. *Journal of Business and Economic Statistics, 7*(3), 363-377.
Barnett, W. A., and de Peretti, P. (2009). Admissible Clustering Of Aggregator Components: A Necessary And Sufficient Stochastic Seminonparametric Test For Weak Separability. *Macroeconomic Dynamics, 13*(S2), 317-334.
Barnett, W. A., Fisher, D., and Serletis, A. (1992). Consumer Theory and the Demand for Money. *Journal of Economic Literature, 30*(4), 2086-2119.
Barnett, W. A., Offenbacher, E. K., and Spindt, P. A. (1984). The new divisia monetary aggregates. *The Journal of Political Economy, 92*(6), 1049.
Beyer, A., Doornik, J. A., and Hendry, D. F. (2000). Constructing Historical Euro-Zone Data: *European University Institute.*
Binner, J. M., Bissoondeeal, R. K., Elger, T., Gazely, A. M., and Mullineux, A. W. (2005). A comparison of linear forecasting models and neural networks: an application to Euro inflation and Euro Divisia. *Applied Economics, 37*(6), 665-680.
Binner, J. M., Bissoondeeal, R. K., Elger, C. T., Jones, B. E., and Mullineux, A. W. (2009). Admissible monetary aggregates for the euro

area. *Journal of International Money and Finance, 28*(1), 99-114.

Binner, J. M., Gazely, A. M., and Kendall, G. (2008). Evaluating the Performance of a Eurodivisia Index Using Artificial Intelligence Techniques. *International Journal of Automation and Computing* 5, (1), 58-62.

Blackorby, C., Russell, R.R. and D. Primont. (1998). Separability: A survey *The Handbook of Utility Theory: S. Barbera, P. Hammond, and C. Seidl eds, Kluwer: Dordrecht., (Vol. 1)*, 49-92.

de Peretti, P. (2005). Testing The Significance Of The Departures From Utility Maximization. *Macroeconomic Dynamics, 9*(03), 372-397.

—. (2007). Testing the Significance of the Departures from Weak Separability. *International Symposia in Economic Theory and Econometrics: Functional Structure Inference, William Barnett and Apostolos Serletis, Eds. Elsevier Press.*

Diewert, W. E. (1976). Exact and superlative index numbers. *Journal of Econometrics, 4*(2), 115-145.

Fisher, I. (1922). The making of index numbers: a study of their varieties, tests, and reliability, *Houghton Mifflin Company.*

Fleissig, A. R., and Whitney, G. A. (2003). A New PC-Based Test for Varian's Weak Separability Conditions. *Journal of Business and Economic Statistics, 21*(1), 133-144.

Fleissig, A. R., and Whitney, G. A. (2005). Testing for the Significance of Violations of Afriat's Inequalities. *Journal of Business and Economic Statistics, 23*(3), 355-362.

Hancock, M. (2005). Divisia Money. *Bank of England Quarterly Bulletin.*

Klein, B. (1974). Competitive Interest Payments on Bank Deposits and the Long-Run Demand for Money. *American Economic Review, 64*(6), 931-949.

Reimers, H.-E. (2002). Analysing Divisia Aggregates for the Euro Area: *Deutsche Bundesbank, Research Centre.*

Startz, R. (1979). Implicit interest on demand deposits. *Journal of Monetary Economics, 5*(4), 515-534.

Stracca, L. (2001). Does liquidity matter? Properties of the synthetic divisia monetary aggregate in the Euro area: *European Central Bank.*

Swofford, J. L., and Whitney, G. A. (1987). Nonparametric Tests of Utility Maximization and Weak Separability for Consumption, Leisure and Money. *The Review of Economics and Statistics, 69*(3), 458-464.

Swofford, J. L., and Whitney, G. A. (1994). A revealed preference test for weakly separable utility maximization with incomplete adjustment. *Journal of Econometrics, 60*(1-2), 235-249.

Theil, H. (1967). Economics and information theory. *Elsevier, Amsterdam.*

Törnqvist, L. (1936). The Bank of Finland's Consumer Price Index. *Bank of Finland Review, 10, 1-8.*
Varian, H. R. (1982). The Nonparametric Approach to Demand Analysis. *Econometrica, 50*(4), 945-973.
—. (1983). Non-Parametric Tests of Consumer Behaviour. *Review of Economic Studies, 50*(1), 99-110.
—. (1985). Non-parametric analysis of optimizing behavior with measurement error. *Journal of Econometrics, 30*, 445-458.

Figure 2-1: Year-Over-Year Growth Rates of the Divisia and Simple-Sum Monetary Aggregates, M1 (Annual Percentage Change)

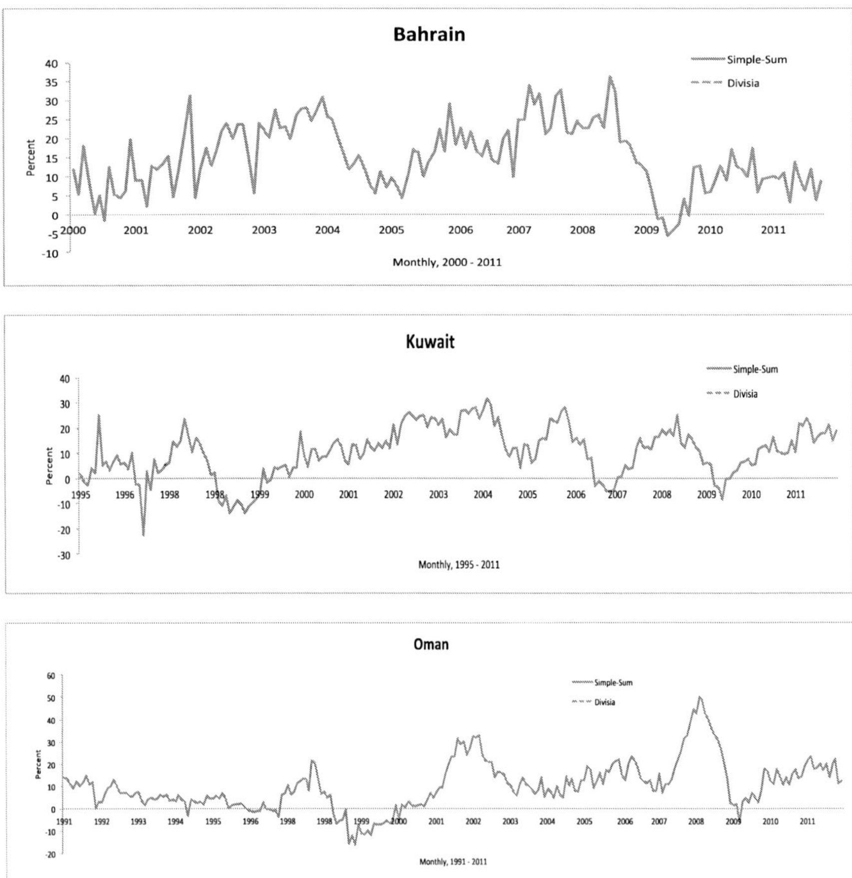

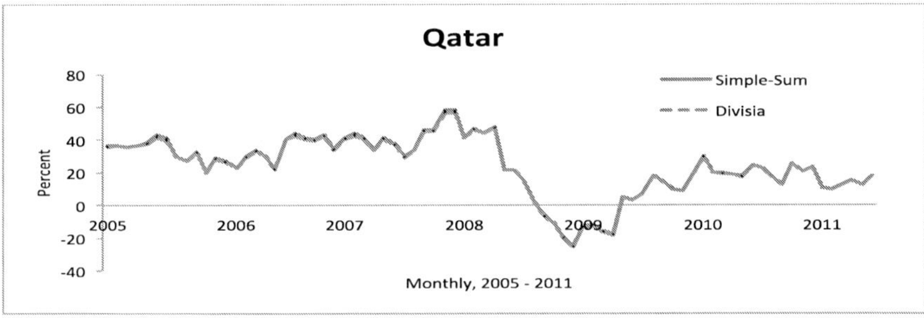
Qatar
Simple-Sum
Divisia
Percent
80
60
40
20
0
-20
-40
2005
2006
2007
2008
2009
2010
2011
Monthly, 2005 - 2011

Saudi Arabia
Simple-Sum
Divisia
Percent
30
25
20
15
10
5
0
2000
2001
2002
2003
2004
2005
2006
2007
2008
2009
2010
2011
2012
Monthly, 2000 - 2011

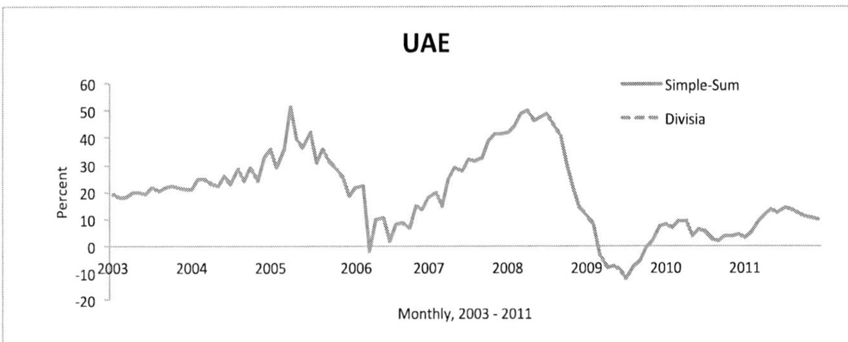
UAE
Simple-Sum
Divisia
Percent
60
50
40
30
20
10
0
-10
-20
2003
2004
2005
2006
2007
2008
2009
2010
2011
Monthly, 2003 - 2011

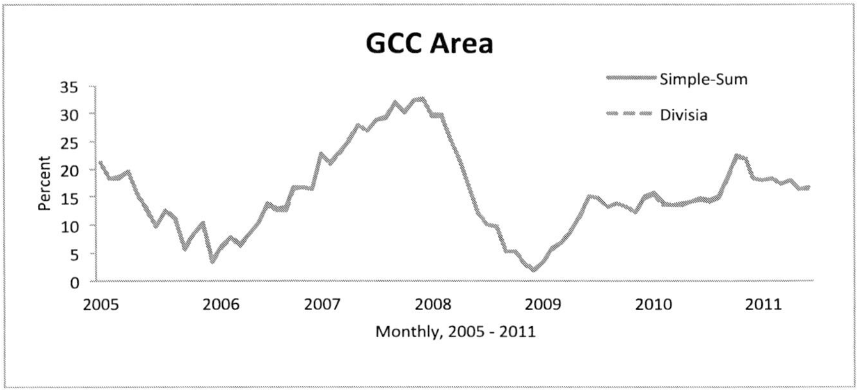

Figure 2-2: Year-Over-Year Growth Rates of the Divisia and Simple-Sum Monetary Aggregates, M2 (Annual Percentage Change)

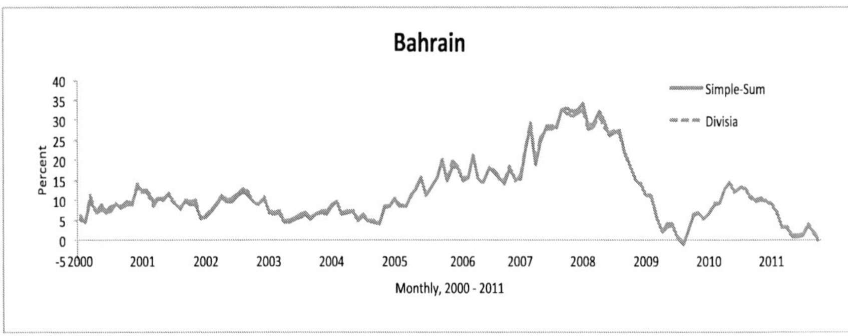

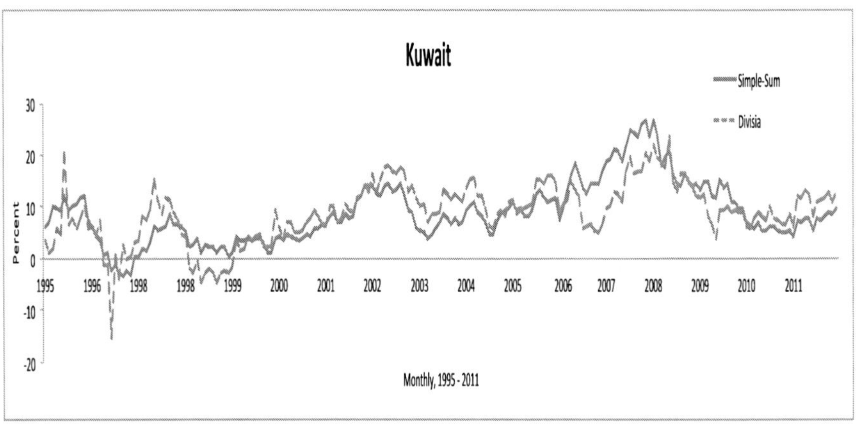

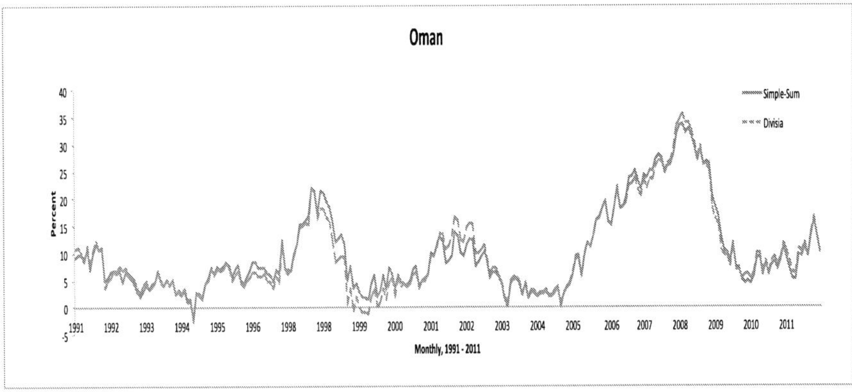
Oman
Simple-Sum
Divisia
Percent
40
35
30
25
20
15
10
5
0
-5
1991
1992
1993
1994
1995
1996
1998
1998
1999
2000
2001
2002
2003
2004
2005
2006
2007
2008
2009
2010
2011
Monthly, 1991 - 2011

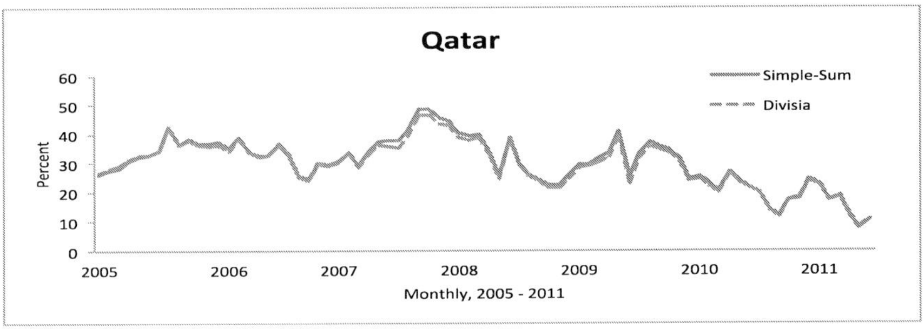
Qatar
Simple-Sum
Divisia
Percent
60
50
40
30
20
10
0
2005
2006
2007
2008
2009
2010
2011
Monthly, 2005 - 2011

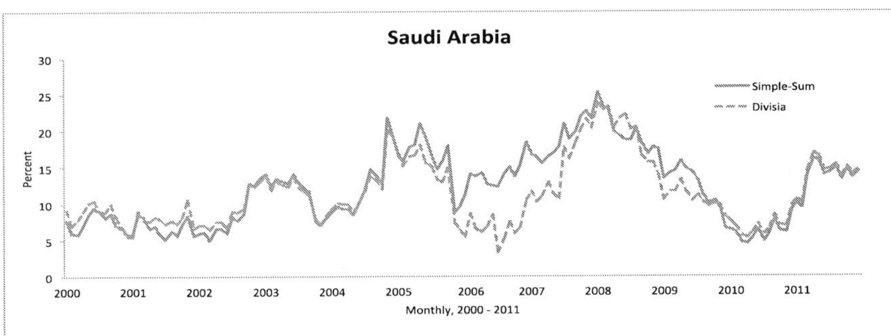
Saudi Arabia
Simple-Sum
Divisia
Percent
30
25
20
15
10
5
0
2000
2001
2002
2003
2004
2005
2006
2007
2008
2009
2010
2011
Monthly, 2000 - 2011

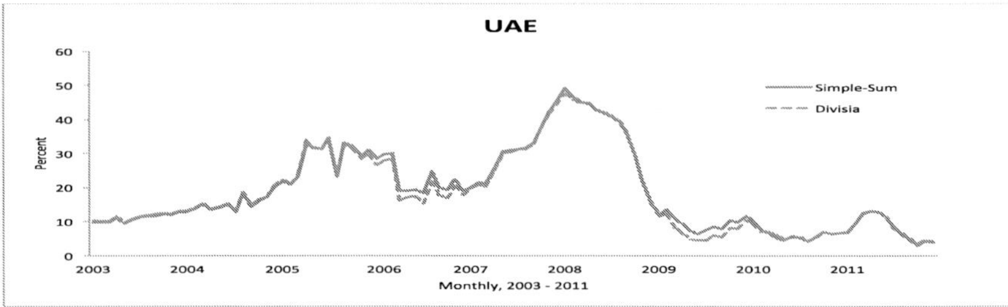
UAE
60
50
40
30
20
10
0
Percent
Simple-Sum
Divisia
2003
2004
2005
2006
2007
2008
2009
2010
2011
Monthly, 2003 - 2011

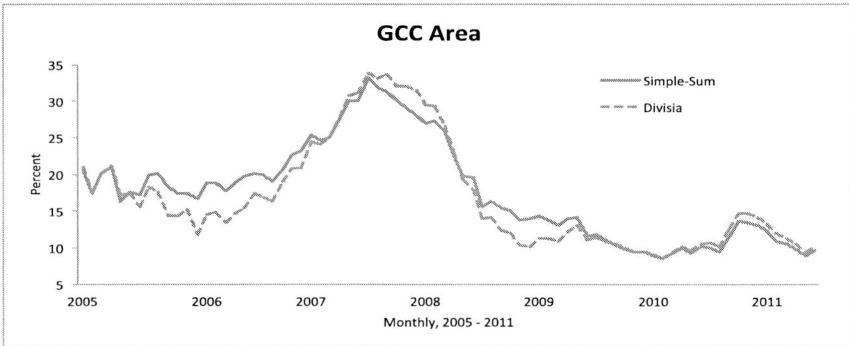
GCC Area
35
30
25
20
15
10
5
Percent
Simple-Sum
Divisia
2005
2006
2007
2008
2009
2010
2011
Monthly, 2005 - 2011

Figure 2-3: User-Cost (Rental) Prices of Monetary Assets

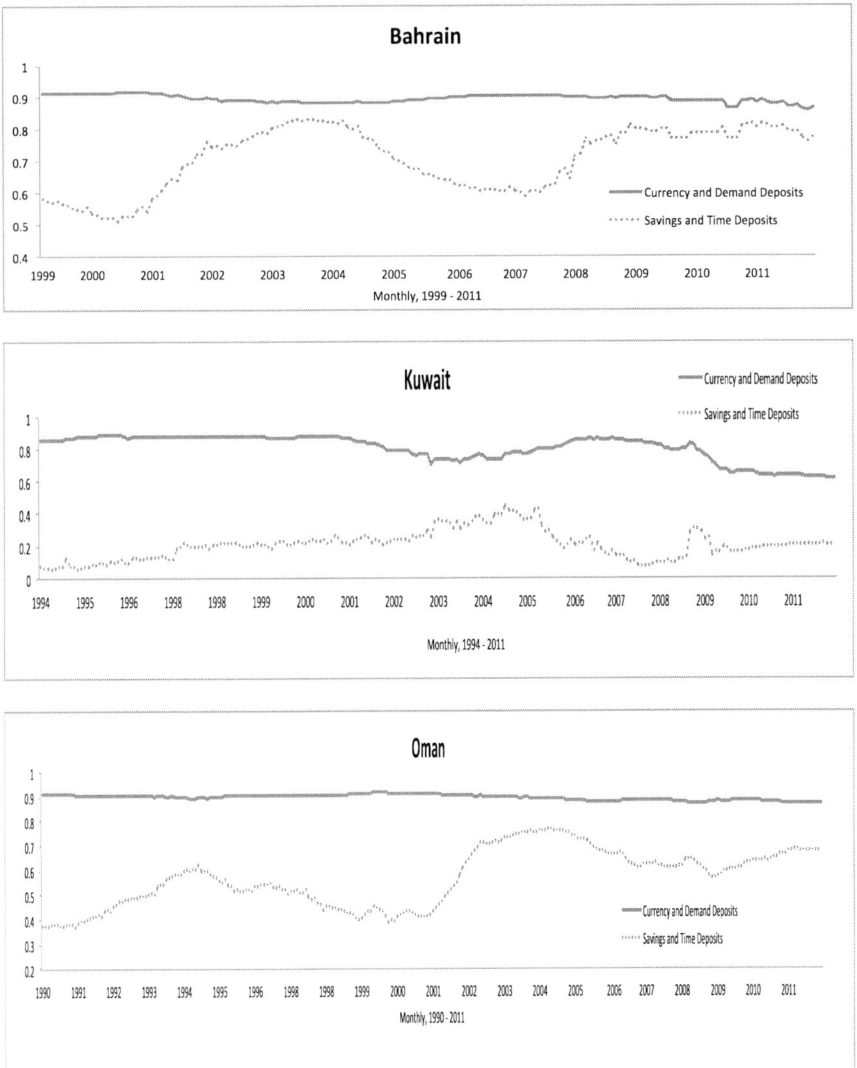

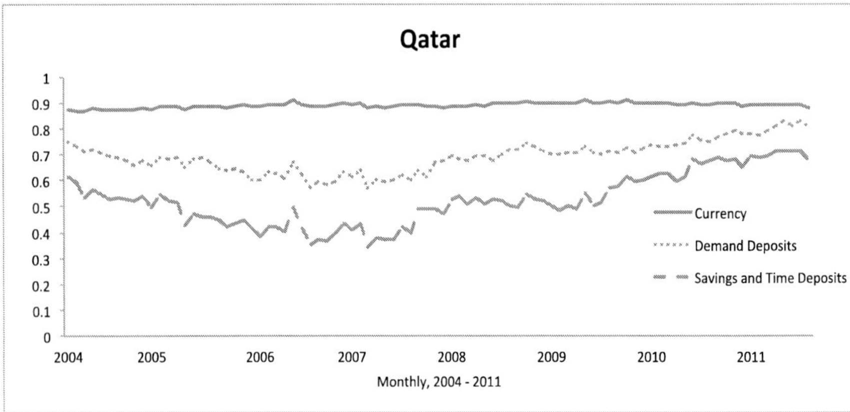
Qatar
1
0.9
0.8
0.7
0.6
0.5
0.4
0.3
0.2
0.1
0
2004
2005
2006
2007
2008
2009
2010
2011
Monthly, 2004 - 2011
Currency
Demand Deposits
Savings and Time Deposits

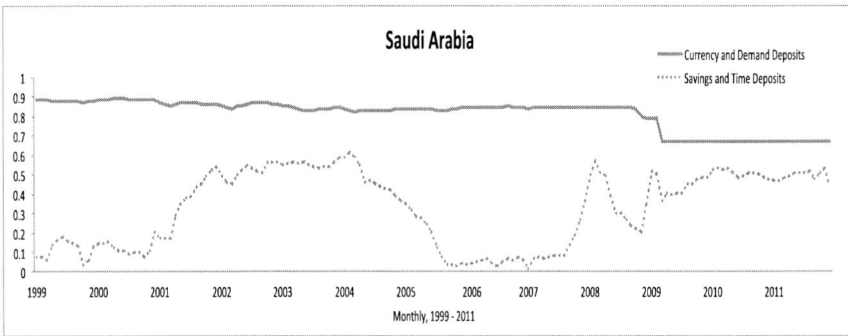
Saudi Arabia
Currency and Demand Deposits
Savings and Time Deposits
1
0.9
0.8
0.7
0.6
0.5
0.4
0.3
0.2
0.1
0
1999
2000
2001
2002
2003
2004
2005
2006
2007
2008
2009
2010
2011
Monthly, 1999 - 2011

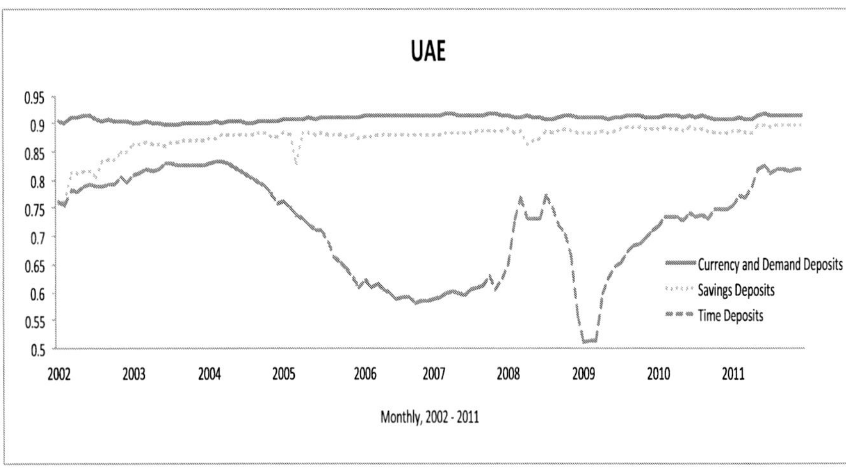
UAE
0.95
0.9
0.85
0.8
0.75
0.7
0.65
0.6
0.55
0.5
2002
2003
2004
2005
2006
2007
2008
2009
2010
2011
Monthly, 2002 - 2011
Currency and Demand Deposits
Savings Deposits
Time Deposits

Figure 2-4: Monthly Growth Rates of the Divisia Aggregate User-Cost Prices for D1 and D2

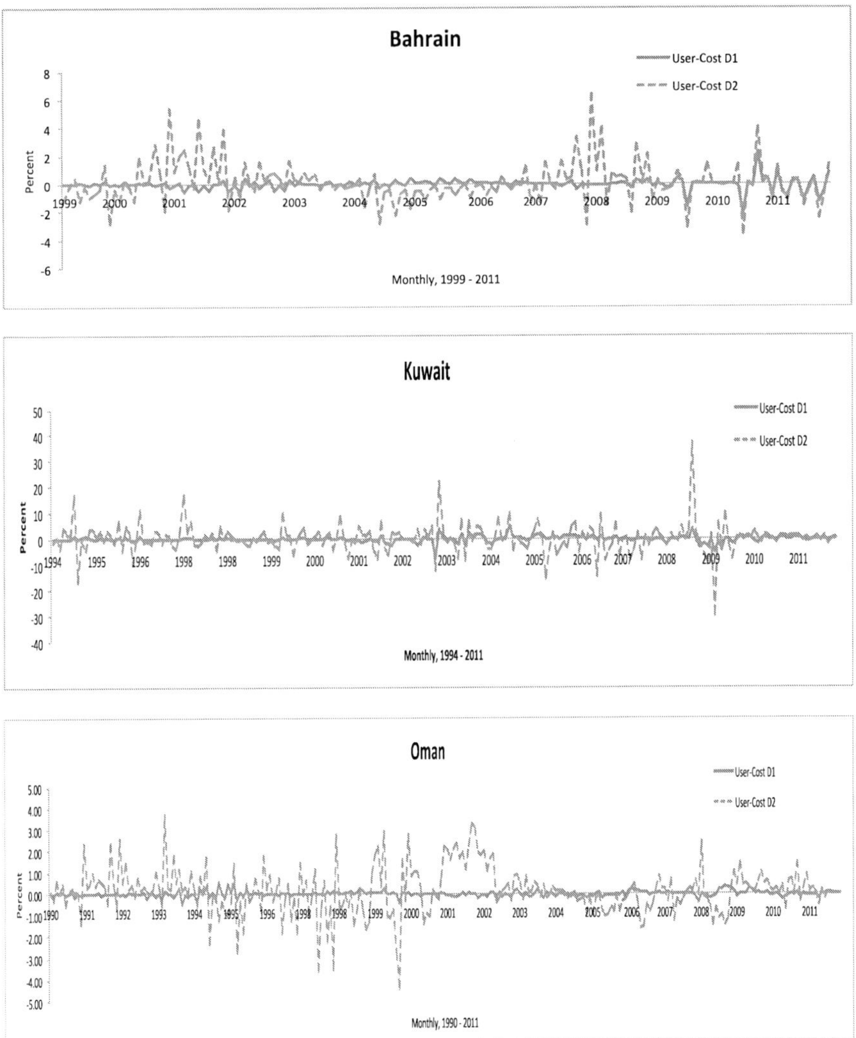

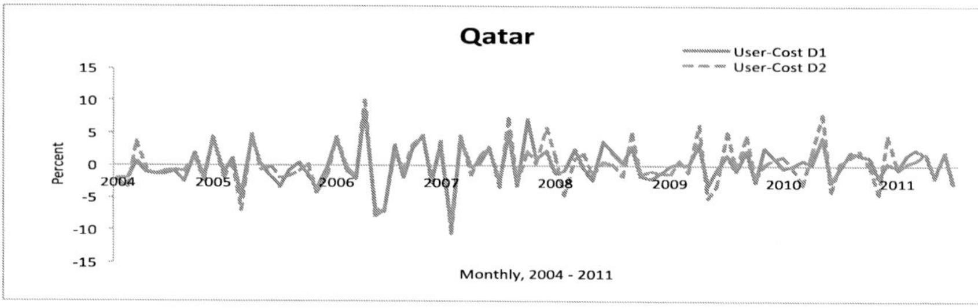
Qatar
User-Cost D1
User-Cost D2
15
10
5
0
-5
-10
-15
Percent
2004
2005
2006
2007
2008
2009
2010
2011
Monthly, 2004 - 2011

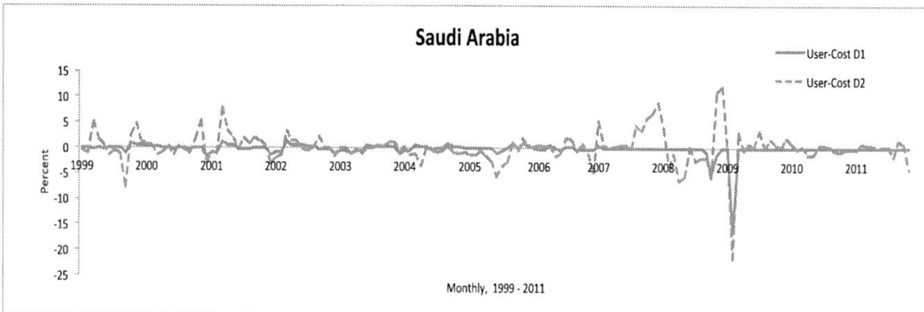
Saudi Arabia
User-Cost D1
User-Cost D2
15
10
5
0
-5
-10
-15
-20
-25
Percent
1999
2000
2001
2002
2003
2004
2005
2006
2007
2008
2009
2010
2011
Monthly, 1999 - 2011

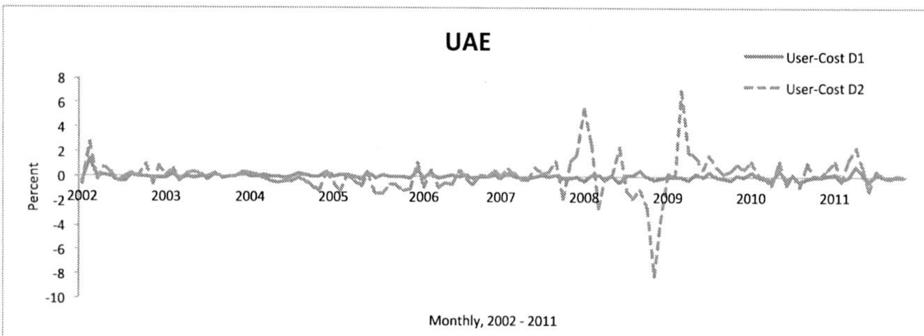
UAE
User-Cost D1
User-Cost D2
8
6
4
2
0
-2
-4
-6
-8
-10
Percent
2002
2003
2004
2005
2006
2007
2008
2009
2010
2011
Monthly, 2002 - 2011

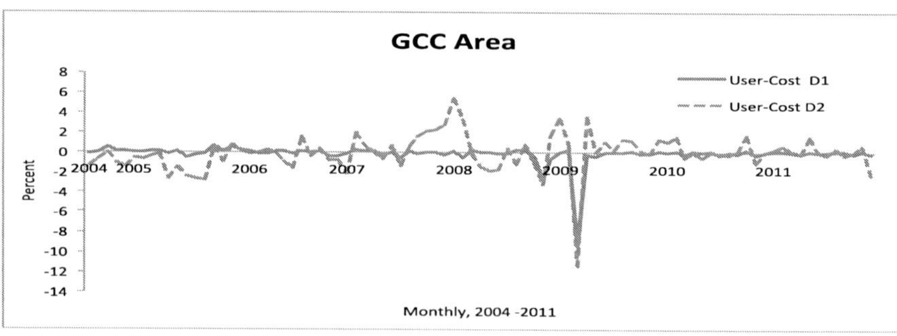
GCC Area
User-Cost D1
User-Cost D2
8
6
4
2
0
-2
-4
-6
-8
-10
-12
-14
Percent
2004
2005
2006
2007
2008
2009
2010
2011
Monthly, 2004 -2011

Figure 2-5: Dual Aggregate User-Cost Prices of the Divisia Monetary Aggregates D1 and D2 (Normalized to 100 in the First Year)

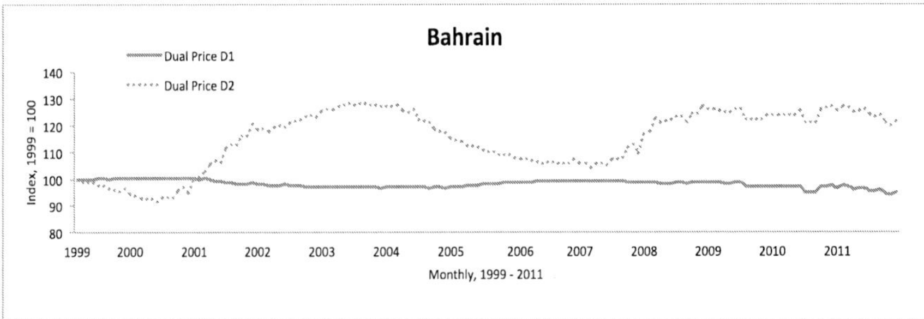

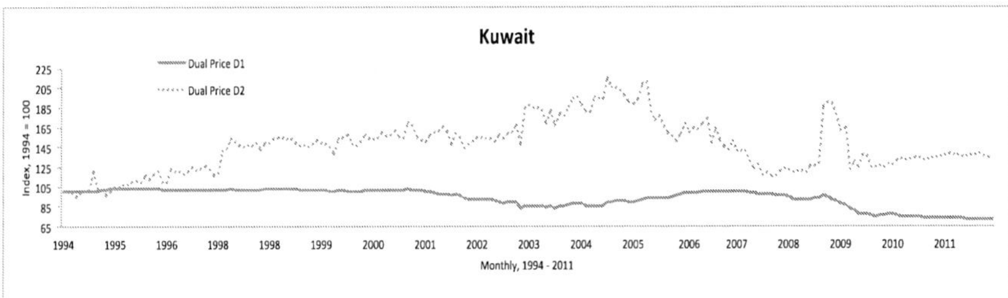

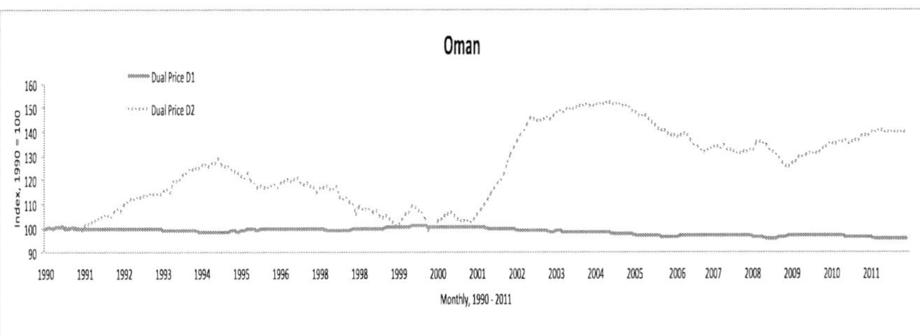

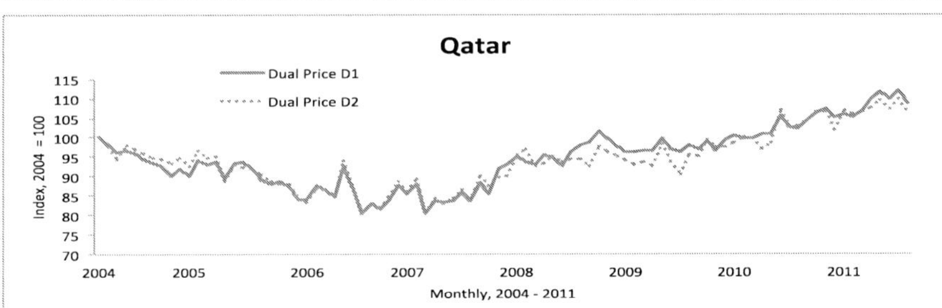

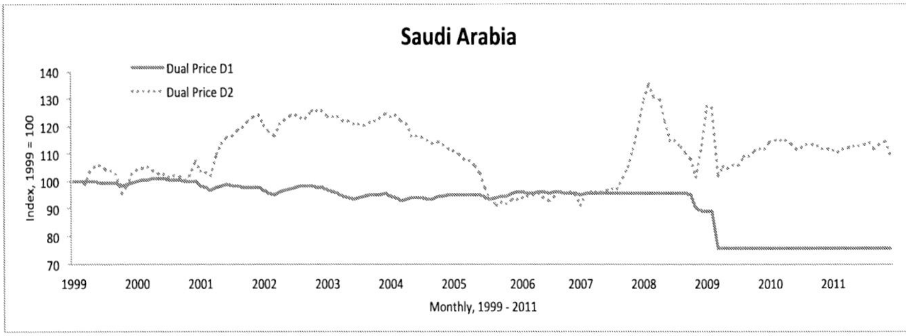
Saudi Arabia
Dual Price D1
Dual Price D2
Index, 1999 = 100
140
130
120
110
100
90
80
70
1999
2000
2001
2002
2003
2004
2005
2006
2007
2008
2009
2010
2011
Monthly, 1999 - 2011

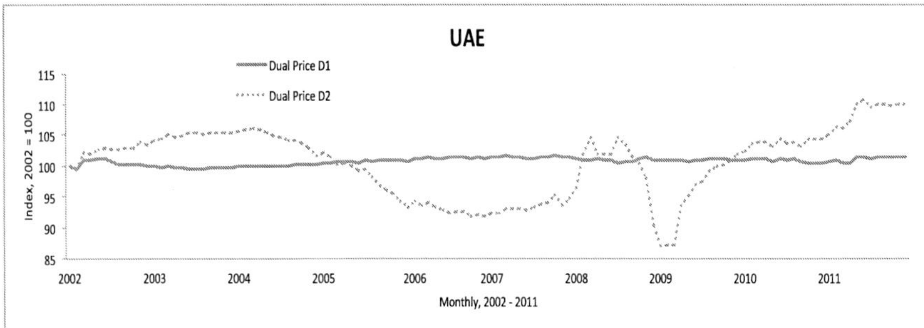
UAE
Dual Price D1
Dual Price D2
Index, 2002 = 100
115
110
105
100
95
90
85
2002
2003
2004
2005
2006
2007
2008
2009
2010
2011
Monthly, 2002 - 2011

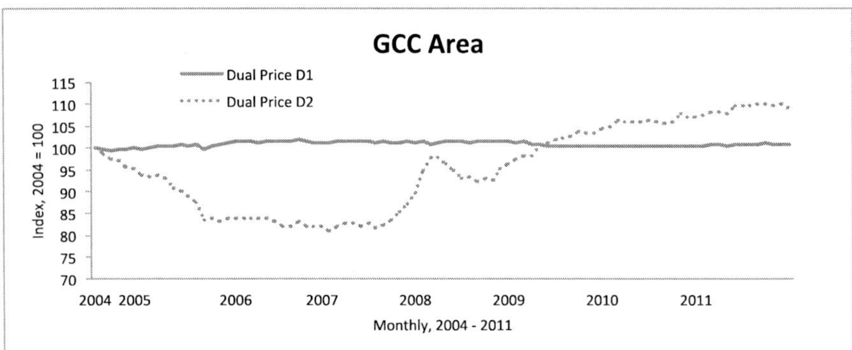
GCC Area
Dual Price D1
Dual Price D2
Index, 2004 = 100
115
110
105
100
95
90
85
80
75
70
2004
2005
2006
2007
2008
2009
2010
2011
Monthly, 2004 - 2011

Figure 2-6: Annualized Interest Rate Aggregates Corresponding to Monetary Assets within M1 and M2

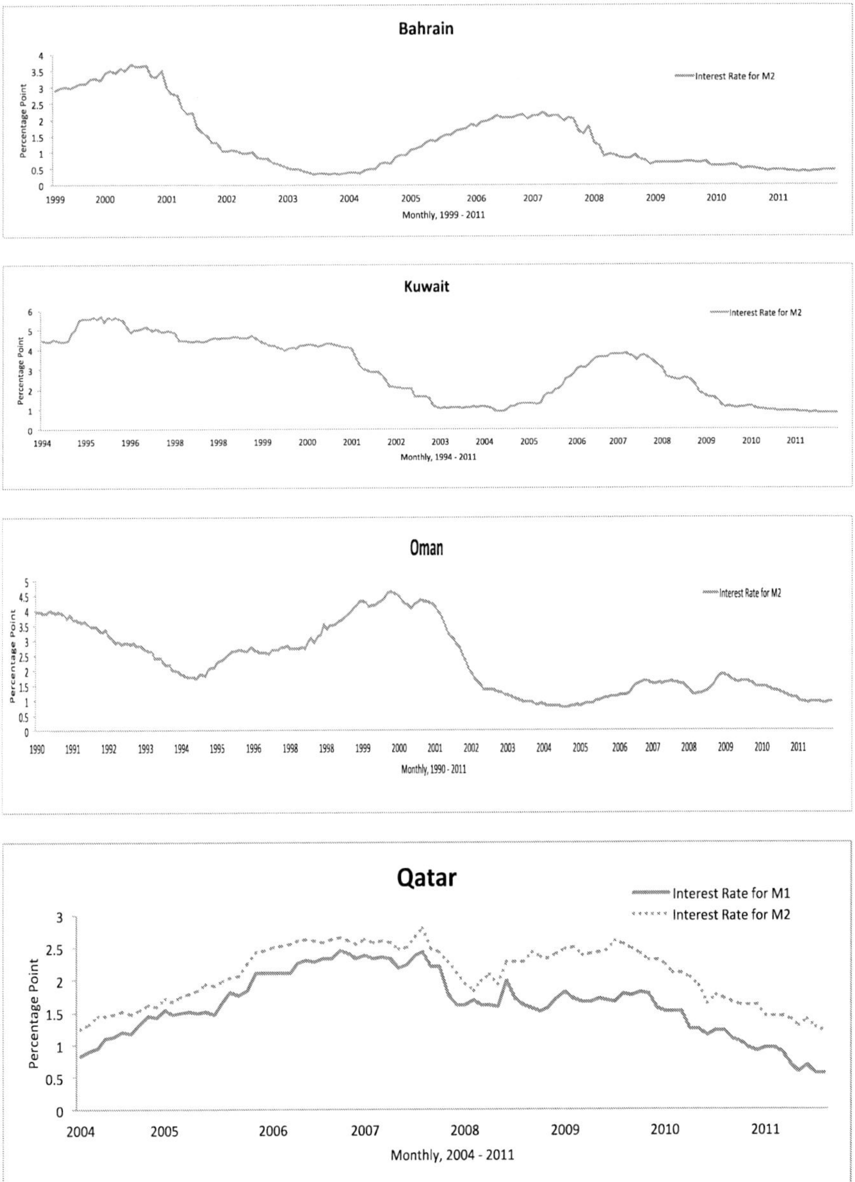

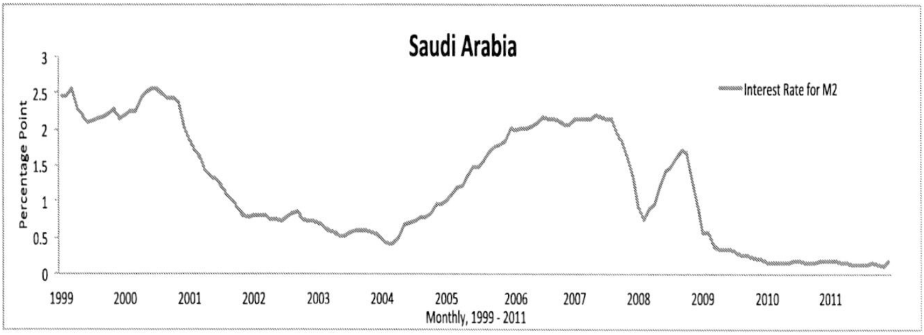
Saudi Arabia
Interest Rate for M2
Percentage Point
3
2.5
2
1.5
1
0.5
0
1999
2000
2001
2002
2003
2004
2005
2006
2007
2008
2009
2010
2011
Monthly, 1999 - 2011

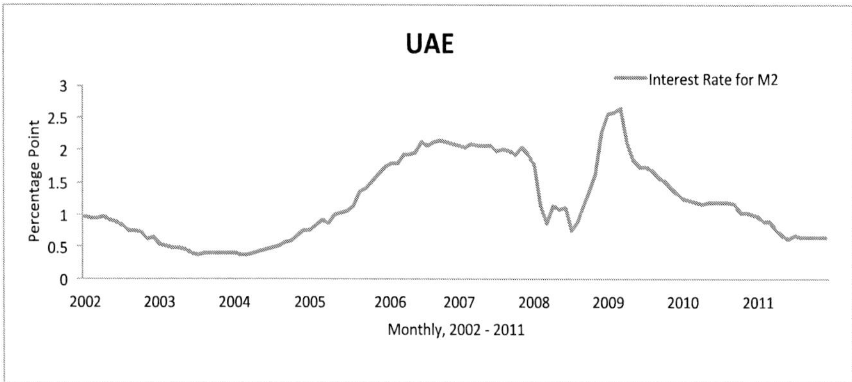
UAE
Interest Rate for M2
Percentage Point
3
2.5
2
1.5
1
0.5
0
2002
2003
2004
2005
2006
2007
2008
2009
2010
2011
Monthly, 2002 - 2011

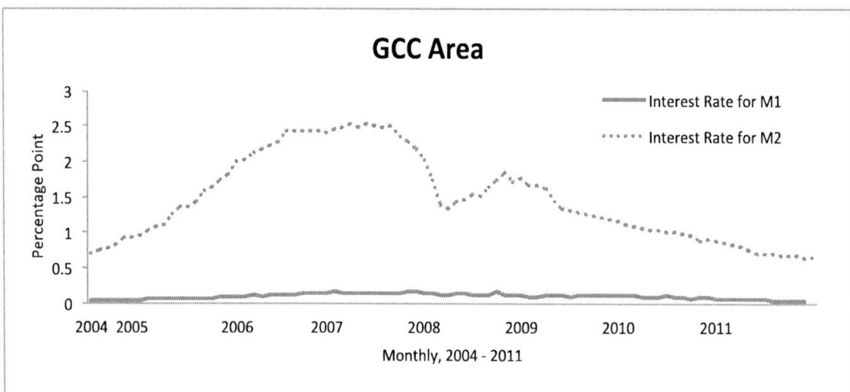
GCC Area
Interest Rate for M1
Interest Rate for M2
Percentage Point
3
2.5
2
1.5
1
0.5
0
2004
2005
2006
2007
2008
2009
2010
2011
Monthly, 2004 - 2011

Figure 2-7: Annual Inflation Rates for the Gulf Area

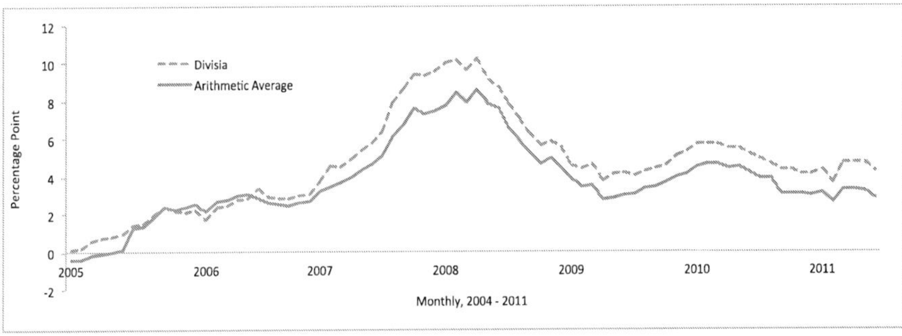

Figure 2-8: Divisia Monetary Services Growth Rate Variances, Ω, of D1 and D2

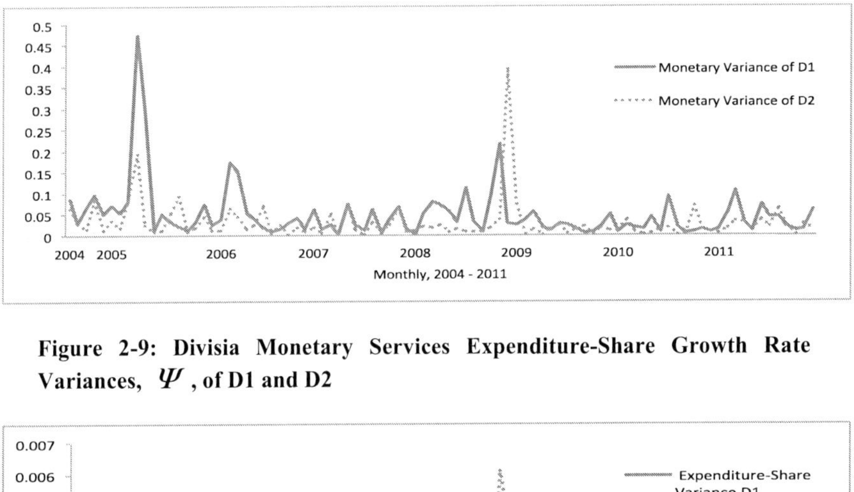

Figure 2-9: Divisia Monetary Services Expenditure-Share Growth Rate Variances, Ψ, of D1 and D2

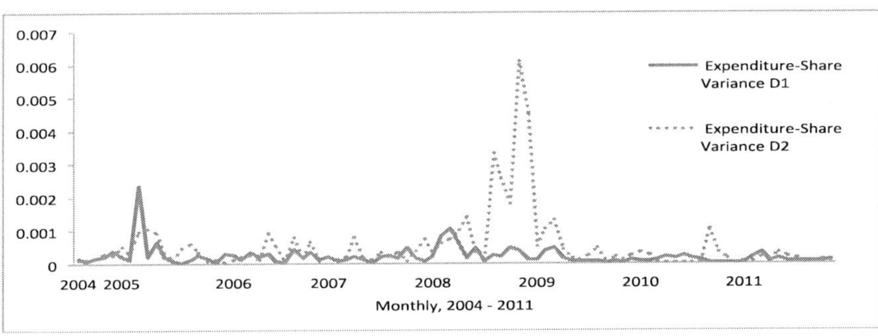

Figure 2-10: Divisia Aggregate User-Cost Growth Rate Variances, Φ, of D1 and D2

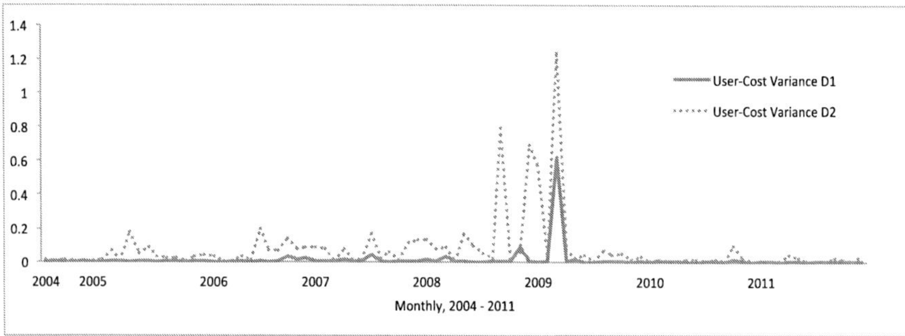

Figure 2-11: Divisia Inflation Rate Variances, Γ_M, of D1 and D2

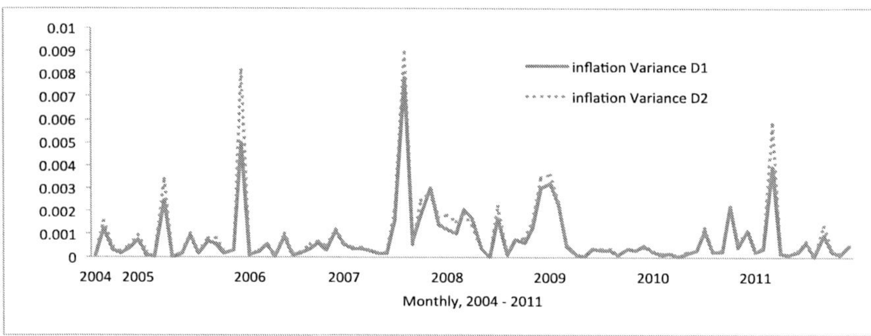

CHAPTER THREE

A COMMON CURRENCY FOR THE GULF STATES: A STOCHASTIC SEMI-NONPARAMETRIC WEAK SEPARABILITY APPROACH

3.1 Introduction

In order to test the feasibility of forming a common currency area, previous studies have approached it using the macro-level measures of Optimum Currency Area (OCA) criteria from Mundell (1961). The OCA criteria include: the factors of mobility, price and wage flexibility, symmetry of shocks, openness, similarity of inflation rates and production structures, financial markets integrability, and the existence of a centralized fiscal policy [see, e.g., McKinnon (1963) and Kenen (1969)]. Several economic unions have adopted similar macro-level criteria to foster economic integration among member countries. For example, the Maastricht criteria (1993) used for joining the European Monetary Union (EMU).

The abovementioned theoretical criteria remain a macro-level measure of the existence of a common currency area. The microeconomic theory—including the consumer theory which explains the optimization behavior pertaining to economic agents—is nonetheless relevant. From the perspective of monetarists, a common currency area exists only when economic agents (and monetary authorities) are unified in terms of what type of asset(s) should be treated as money [Swofford (2000)]. In particular, if all economic agents within an economic union perceive the same asset(s) as money, a common monetary aggregate exists for the whole union.

A key theoretical condition for the existence of admissible monetary aggregates is the weak separability of the utility function [Binner, Bissoondeeal, Elger, Jones, and Mullineux (2009)]. The weak separability of the monetary aggregator function (micro function) nested in a utility function from all other arguments in that utility function indicates the existence of an optimum currency. Indeed, optimum currency area refers to not only a single country, but also to multiple countries.[1] Numerous studies have applied the weak separability tests on various applications to examine the admissibility condition for asset groupings. These studies include: Varian (1982, 1983, and 1985), Swofford (2000), Fleissig and Whitney (2003, 2005, and 2008), Swofford and Whitney (1987, 1994), Barnett and Choi (1989), de Peretti (2005, 2007), Barnett and Peretti (2009), and Binner, Bissoondeeal, Elger, Jones, and Mullineux (2009).

Admissibility for monetary aggregates has not yet been fully defined. Barnett (1982) discusses the admissibility concept in light of selecting the optimal monetary aggregate for which admissible groups of monetary assets have to be weakly separable from all other arguments nested in a utility function. Barnett and de Peretti (2009) linked the admissibility to the microeconomic condition in which the marginal rate of substitution between any two monetary assets inside a group is independent from all other assets outside that group. Henceforth, in this paper, admissible clustering of assets refers to groups of monetary assets that are weakly separable from all other assets nested in a utility function.

The four central banks of the GCC countries—Bahrain, Kuwait, Qatar, and Saudi Arabia—have decided to launch a common currency by 2015 where an indivisible monetary policy will be uniformly implemented on all member states.[2] A common currency area mandates not only that all member countries abandon their national currencies, but also that they follow a single GCC-wide monetary policy.[3] The existence of a common currency in the Gulf area also implies that monetary assets with similar characteristics can be clustered together as suggested by monetary aggregation and microeconomic theory. For monetary policy in the Gulf area to be effective, policy makers need to identify the differences between monetary assets of the individual countries.

All GCC central banks classify currency in circulation and demand deposits as the components of the narrow monetary aggregate, namely $M1$. The broader monetary aggregate, $M2$, incorporates monetary

---

[1] An example of an optimum currency area for a single country is the United States where all states adopt the U.S. dollar as the national currency whereas the European monetary union exemplifies the optimum currency area for multinational countries.

[2] Oman and UAE have opted out of the Gulf Monetary Union (GMU). Oman has not met the convergence criteria required for joining the GMU whereas the UAE disputes the GMC being headquartered in Riyadh, the capital of Saudi Arabia.

[3] See Mundell (1961) and McKinnon (1963) for more details regarding the theoretical background of an Optimal Currency Area.

assets within $M1$ as well as less liquid assets such as savings and time deposits. While GCC central banks have a unified definition of monetary aggregates, the monetary components per se may not provide the same monetary services. For instance, demand deposits in Qatar which offer positive interest rates may provide different monetary services than demand deposits in the rest of the Gulf countries where demand deposits offer zero interest rates. Hence, it is important to assess whether it is permissible to aggregate demand deposits with zero interest rates with other demand deposits that bear interest.

The similarity in interest rates does not necessarily guarantee the existence of admissible groupings of monetary assets. For example, countries' idiosyncratic shocks and benchmark rates are all factors that determine the compatibility of clustering monetary assets within an aggregate. Policy makers ought to use admissible groupings of monetary assets to properly construct their monetary aggregates.

The primary goals of this paper are to provide an admissible clustering of monetary assets within the Gulf countries and produce admissible monetary aggregates for the overall GCC area. We use the Optimal Currency Area criteria based upon microeconomics and economic aggregation theory. We investigate the feasibility of a common currency for the GCC area by testing the weak separability of monetary assets within the Gulf area. We perform a twofold weak separability test: first, we apply the weak separability test on monetary assets within countries. This allows us to build admissible monetary aggregates for all GCC countries. Afterwards, we test the weak separability of monetary assets within specific monetary aggregates across GCC countries. If the data pass the weak separability test, a common currency area exists.

Although the Gulf monetary union currently comprises only four member GCC countries, we carry out the empirical tests for all GCC countries to not only test the feasibility for non-member countries joining the monetary union but also to provide broader insight about the monetary policy in the Gulf region. Our findings from testing the weak separability of monetary assets within the GCC countries suggest that the broad monetary aggregates for all countries are weakly separable from total private consumption (and hence the existence of $M2$). In addition, components of $M1$ (i.e. currency in circulation and demand deposits) are weak separable from the other less liquid monetary assets, namely quasi-money and savings and time deposits. However, our weak separability test indicates that demand deposits in Qatar (which offer positive interest rates) cannot be included in $M1$ and hence currency in circulation for Qatar will be the only monetary asset included in the narrow monetary aggregate.

For the existence of the GCC area monetary aggregates, our weak separability test reports the existence of the broad monetary aggregate $M2$. Specifically, we find that monetary assets for all GCC countries are weakly separable from the GCC area consumption. Interestingly, narrow monetary aggregate does not exist for the GCC area and hence the six countries cannot form a common currency area. If we exclude Oman from the monetary union, the remaining countries form a common currency area where $M2$ exists and $M1$ is weakly separable from *M2*. The five remaining countries—Bahrain, Kuwait, Qatar, Saudi Arabia, and United Arab Emirates—form a common currency area.

Using the admissible groups of monetary assets, we construct Divisia monetary aggregates for the Gulf area recursively by first building the Divisia monetary indexes for the GCC countries and then aggregate across countries. We find that the gap between Divisia and simple-sum growth rates widened during times of high uncertainty such as the financial crises. Specifically, the Divisia growth rates are low prior to recessions, while those growth rates increase at a faster pace than simple-sum during recoveries [Alkhareif and Barnett (2012)].

Prior to the European sovereign debt crises, Binner, Bissoondeeal, Elger, Jones, and Mullineux (2009) reported the weak separability of the monetary aggregates $M2$ and $M3$ for the Euro area over the period from 1980 to 2005 by using Fleissig and Whitney (2003) weak separability test. Nevertheless, it is worthwhile to re-examine the admissibility of the monetary aggregates in the Eurozone especially during the financial crises. Further research pertaining to the European states could make use of the stochastic semi-nonparametric test for weak separability introduced by Barnett and de Peretti (2009) to examine the weak separability of the euro monetary aggregates during times of high uncertainty and periods of economic disruptions, such as the financial turmoil.

The chapter is structured as follows. Section 3.2 provides the theoretical background and describes our weak separability test. Section 3.3 describes the data used in this paper and briefly discusses the method of constructing Divisia consumption aggregates for the Gulf area. Section 3.4 presents the empirical results pertaining to each single county and for the Gulf area. Section 3.5 constructs Divisia monetary aggregates for the GCC area. Section 3.6 comprises the conclusion.

3.2 Methodology

Although all GCC central banks use currency and demand deposits as money, no aggregator function exists for those assets (i.e., countries do not form a common currency area) unless all of the countries' currencies and demand deposits satisfy the weak separability test. It is worthwhile to investigate, for instance, whether demand deposits in Qatar which offer positive interest rates can be consolidated with the other countries' zero-bearing assets such as currency and demand deposits. In fact, it is possible that countries' zero-bearing assets cannot form an aggregate for other reasons such as differences in their benchmark rates or idiosyncratic shocks. Therefore, weak separability test enables us to identify whether or not a set of monetary assets form a common currency area.

This section gives an overview of the traditional nonparametric tests of utility maximization proposed by Varian (1982, 1983, and 1985) as well as the stochastic semi-nonparametric test for weak separability introduced by Barnett and de Peretti (2009). Both tests are based upon the General Axiom of Revealed Preference (GARP). This latter method for testing weak separability exploits the microeconomic condition in which the marginal rate of substitution between goods within a group is independent of goods outside the group.

3.2.1 The Nonparametric Test for Weak Separability

Let **X** be a $(T \times k)$ matrix of total private consumption, **C**, and monetary assets, **M,** where T denotes the number of observations and k denotes the number of goods. Let **M** be a $(T \times a)$ matrix and **C** be a $(T \times (k-a))$ matrix, where $a \in \{1,...,k-1\}$. Let **P** be the $(T \times k)$ corresponding prices where the price of a monetary asset is called the user cost of that asset.[4] In particular, let $\boldsymbol{\Pi}$ and $\mathbf{P}^c$ be the corresponding price matrices of **M** and **C,** respectively. Let $\mathbf{x}_j = (x_{j1}, x_{j2}, ..., x_{jk})'$ and $\boldsymbol{p}_j = (p_{j1}, p_{j2}, ..., p_{jk})'$ denote the jth $(j = 1,...,T)$ rows of **X** and **P**. Denote $\boldsymbol{m}_j = (m_{j1}, m_{j2}, ..., m_{ja})'$ and $\boldsymbol{c}_j = (c_{j(a+1)}, c_{j(a+2)}, ..., c_{jk})'$ as the jth rows of **M** and **C,**

[4] Barnett (1978; 1980a,b; and 1987) derived the Jorgensonian user cost of monetary assets from a rigorous Fisherine intertemporal consumption expenditure allocation model.

respectively. Similarly, denote $\boldsymbol{p}_j^c = (p_{j(a+1)}^c, p_{j(a+2)}^c, \dots, p_{jk}^c)'$ and $\boldsymbol{\pi}_j = (\pi_{j1}, \pi_{j2}, \dots, \pi_{ja})'$ as the jth rows of $\mathbf{P}^c$ and $\boldsymbol{\Pi}$.

Formally, the weak separability of a monetary aggregate $\mathbf{M}_i = f(\mathbf{m}_i), i = 1, \dots, T,$ in the utility function $U()$ can be written as follows:

$$U(\mathbf{x}_i) = V(\mathbf{c}_i, f(\mathbf{m}_i)) \tag{3.1}$$

where $V()$ is a strictly increasing macro function and $f()$ is a sub-utility (micro) function. The existence of $U(), V(),$ and $f()$ is essential for weak separablility to hold between arguments within a utility function as indicated by Barnett and de Peretti (2009).

Varian (1982, 1983) has proposed a nonparametric procedure for testing weak separability that relies on the Generalized Axiom of Revealed Preference (GARP). Consider the following binary relations: $\mathbf{x}_i$ is strictly directly revealed preferred to $\mathbf{x}_j$, written $\mathbf{x}_i\mathbf{P}^o\mathbf{x}_j$, if $\mathbf{p}_i \cdot \mathbf{x}_i > \mathbf{p}_i \cdot \mathbf{x}_j$; $\mathbf{x}_i$ is directly revealed preferred to $\mathbf{x}_j$, written $\mathbf{x}_i\mathbf{R}^o\mathbf{x}_j$, if $\mathbf{p}_i \cdot \mathbf{x}_i \geq \mathbf{p}_i \cdot \mathbf{x}_j$; and $\mathbf{x}_i$ is revealed preferred to $\mathbf{x}_j$, written $\mathbf{x}_i\mathbf{R}\mathbf{x}_j$, if $\mathbf{x}_i\mathbf{R}^o\mathbf{x}_s, \mathbf{x}_s\mathbf{R}^o\mathbf{x}_r, \dots, \mathbf{x}_q\mathbf{R}^o\mathbf{x}_j$, where $\mathbf{R}$ is the transitive closure of $\mathbf{R}^o$.[5]

Given the abovementioned binary relations, Varian (1982, 1983) defined GARP as follows: a set of data $\{(\boldsymbol{x}_i, \boldsymbol{p}_i), (\boldsymbol{x}_j, \boldsymbol{p}_j)\}_{i,j=1}^{T}$ satisfies GARP if $\mathbf{x}_i\mathbf{R}\mathbf{x}_j$ implies not $\mathbf{x}_j\mathbf{P}^o\mathbf{x}_i$ for $i, j = 1, \dots, T$. That is, $\mathbf{x}_i\mathbf{R}\mathbf{x}_j$ implies that $\mathbf{p}_j \cdot \mathbf{x}_j \leq \mathbf{p}_j \cdot \mathbf{x}_i$ for all $i \in \{1, \dots, T\}, j \in \{1, \dots, T\}$.[6] Clearly, GARP is a necessary and sufficient condition for a data set to be consistent with utility maximization and hence the existence of a well-behaved utility function [Serletis (2001)]. For a data set $\{(\boldsymbol{x}_i, \boldsymbol{p}_i)\}_{i=1}^{T}$, Varian (1982 and 1983)

---

[5] See de Peretti (2005) for more details about the properties of the matrices $\mathbf{P}^0$, $\mathbf{R}^0$, and $\mathbf{R}$.

[6] See Barnett and de Peretti (2009) for more details regarding the definition of GARP.

showed that the existence of a locally nonsatiated utility function $U()$ that rationalizes the data is indeed equivalent to the condition within which there exist utility indexes U_i and marginal income indexes λ_i, where $U_i, \lambda_i > 0, i \in \{1,...,T\}$, that satisfy the Afriat inequalities:

$$U_i \leq U_j + \lambda_j \mathbf{p}_j \cdot (\mathbf{x}_i - \mathbf{x}_j), \tag{3.2}$$

for $i, j = 1,...,T$.

As pointed out by Barnett and de Peretti (2009), testing for the weak separability of the aggregator function, $\mathbf{M}_i = f(\mathbf{m}_i), i = 1,...,T,$ requires the following conditions to hold:

(i) The data set $\{(\boldsymbol{m}_i, \boldsymbol{\pi}_i)\}_{i=1}^{T}$ satisfies GARP and hence the existence of the sub-utility (aggregator) function $f()$.

(ii) The data set $\{(\boldsymbol{c}_i, \boldsymbol{p}_i^c), (\boldsymbol{m}_i, \boldsymbol{\pi}_i)\}_{i=1}^{T}$ satisfies GARP and hence the existence of the overall utility function $U()$.

(iii) The data set $\{(\boldsymbol{c}_i, U_i), (\boldsymbol{p}_i^c, \lambda_i^{-1})\}_{i=1}^{T}$ satisfies GARP.

Since the indexes U_i, λ_i satisfy the above-mentioned Afriat inequalities for the subset $\{(\boldsymbol{m}_i, \boldsymbol{\pi}_i)\}_{i=1}^{T}$, the monetary aggregator function $f(\mathbf{m}_i), i = 1,...,T$, is weakly separable in the overall utility function $U()$. However, the above test is nonstochastic, which implies that a single violation of GARP, even when the violation is purely due to measurement error, will lead to a rejection of the weak separability. To overcome this problem, Varian (1985) has developed a stochastic nonparametric test in which the true data are assumed to be consistent with the optimization behavior, but unobservable. In particular, the unobserved data are linked to their observed counterparts via normally distributed error terms with zero mean and constant variance. Varian's nonparametric test consists of first, finding the minimal adjustment needed for the data to satisfy Afriat inequalities; second, determining the significance of violation.

de Peretti (2005) outlined two major drawbacks with this approach. First, the procedure is computationally burdensome and it requires some prior knowledge regarding the variance of the true errors—which is generally unknown. Second, not only is the power of the test unknown, but also the procedure can be misleading especially under the alternative.[7]

3.2.2 A Stochastic Semi-Nonparametric Test for Weak Separability

Barnett and de Peretti (2009) proposed a new procedure which not only tests the significance of violation of GARP, but also replaces the Afriat inequalities condition (which is only a sufficient condition) with a necessary and sufficient one. Since the real world is not deterministic and hence the extensions to risk are relevant, we assume that quantities (i.e., total private consumption and monetary assets) are not directly observed but rather measured with error. Under the null, the unobservable quantities are generated by a weakly separable utility function, but it is measured with error [Barnett and de Peretti (2009)]:

$$\mathbf{x}_i = \mathbf{x}_i^* + \boldsymbol{\psi}_i \tag{3.3}$$

for $i = 1,...,T$, where $\mathbf{x}_i^*$ is a vector of unobservable quantities while $\boldsymbol{\psi}_i$ is a vector of the measurment errors.[8] Following Barnett and de Peretti (2009), we assume that the measurment error is normally distributed with zero mean and variance $\sigma_{\psi i}^2$.

It is worth mentioning that the traditional nonstochastic models are more likely to produce type 1 errors because the weak separability will be rejected whenever violations of GARP appear, regardless of their significance. Barnett and Choi (1989) described a bias toward higher rejection of the weak separability since the traditional nonstochastic models will reject the weak separability even though the violations are due to measurement and stochastic errors.[9] To overcome this problem, we extend our model to the stochastic case to determine the significant of violations when testing the data for GARP. In particular, we extend model (3.1) to the stochastic case where, for $i = 1,...,T$, variables are measured with error:

---

[7] See Barnett and Choi (1989), de Peretti (2005), and Varian (1985) for a more complete discussion.

[8] Throughout this chapter, the asterisk indicates that the variable is unobservable.

[9] See Barnett and Choi (1989) as well as Barnett and de Peretti (2009) for a more complete discussion.

$$U(\mathbf{x}_i^*) = V(\mathbf{c}_i^*, f(\mathbf{m}_i^*)), \tag{3.4}$$

The model's framework enables us to distinguish between significant versus nonsignificant violations of GARP used in conditions (i) and (ii). The nonsignificant violations of GARP occur when the data fail to pass the GARP test due to purely stochastic factors such as measurement error. Therefore, the rejection of the weak separability must result from significant violations of GARP.

The existence of the sub-utility function and the overall utility function requires that the data sets $\{(\boldsymbol{m}_i, \boldsymbol{\pi}_i)\}_{i=1}^T$ and $\{(\boldsymbol{c}_i, \boldsymbol{p}_i^c), (\boldsymbol{m}_i, \boldsymbol{\pi}_i)\}_{i=1}^T$ respectively pass the GARP test. Whenever violations appear, we test for their significance. Based upon de Peretti (2005, 2007), Barnett and de Peretti (2009) developed a procedure that measures the significance of the violations of GARP when testing for weak separability. The procedure consists of finding the minimal adjustment required for the data to satisfies GARP [i.e., the data is consistent with conditions (i) and (ii)]. Mathematically, computing the minimal adjustment is achieved by solving the following quadratic program over z_{ij}:

$$obj = \min_{z_{ij}} \sum_{i=1}^{T} \sum_{j=1}^{k} (x_{ij} - z_{ij})^2 \tag{3.5}$$

subject to

$$\mathbf{z}_i \mathbf{R} \mathbf{z}_j \Rightarrow \mathbf{p}_j \cdot \mathbf{z}_j \le \mathbf{p}_j \cdot \mathbf{z}_i$$

$$\forall i \in \{1,...,T\} \forall j \in \{1,...,T\}$$

$$\mathbf{z}_i^m \mathbf{R} \mathbf{z}_j^m \Rightarrow \pi_j \cdot \mathbf{z}_j^m \le \pi_j \cdot \mathbf{z}_j^m$$

where $\boldsymbol{z}_h^m = (z_{h1}, z_{h2}, \dots, z_{ha})'$ for $h = i, j$.

Denote $\widehat{\mathbf{Z}}$ as the matrix solution to (3.5) and let $\widehat{\boldsymbol{\Omega}} = \mathbf{X} - \widehat{\mathbf{Z}}$ be the $(T \times k)$ matrix of theoretical residuals. Similarly, define $\boldsymbol{\Psi} = \mathbf{X} - \mathbf{X}^*$ as the $(T \times k)$ matrix of the measurement error—which is generally unknown and hence has to be estimated by a suitable econometrical technique. Our goal is to incorporate the measurement error with the theoretical residuals in a way that enables us to measure the significance of violation of GARP. Barnett and de Peretti (2009) proposed the following procedure. For good $j, j=1,...,k,$ denote $\widehat{\mathbf{\Omega}_{.j}} = (\hat{\omega}_{1j}, \hat{\omega}_{2j}, ..., \hat{\omega}_{Tj})$ as the jth column of $\widehat{\mathbf{\Omega}}$. Let $\widehat{Max_j} = max(\widehat{\mathbf{\Omega}_{.j}})$ and $\widehat{Min_j} = min(\widehat{\mathbf{\Omega}_{.j}})$. Similarly, Denote $\boldsymbol{\psi}_{.j} = (\psi_{1j}, \psi_{2j}, ..., \psi_{Tj})$ as the jth column of $\mathbf{\Psi}$. Let $Max_j = max(\boldsymbol{\psi}_{.j})$ and $Min_j = min(\boldsymbol{\psi}_{.j})$. The following Fisher-Tippett theorem holds, given our specifications of the measurement error:

Let $\boldsymbol{\psi}_{.j} = (\psi_{1j}, \psi_{2j}, ..., \psi_{Tj})$ be an iid sequence of random variables. If there exist numbers $a_j \in R$, $b_j > 0$, and

$$(Max_j - a_j)b_j^{-1} \xrightarrow{\mathcal{L}} G,$$

where G is a nondegenerate distribution function, then G belongs to one of the following standard Extreme Value Distribution (EVD) functions:[10]

Gumbel (*type I*): $G(x) = exp\left[-exp(-x)\right], x \in R$

Fréchet (*type II*): $G(x) = \begin{cases} exp(-x^{-\alpha_j}), & x > 0, \alpha_j > 0 \\ 0, & x \leq 0 \end{cases}$

Weibull (*type III*): $G(x) = \begin{cases} exp\left[-(-x^{\alpha_j})\right], & x \leq 0, \alpha_j > 0 \\ 1, & x > 0 \end{cases}$

Barnett and de Peretti (2009) stated that it is possible to determine the domain of attraction pertaining to the distribution law of the extremes, given a prior knowledge about the true distribution of the errors. Under

---

[10] To avoid redundancy, we report the Fisher-Tippett theorem for only the largest extremes. Similar outcomes follow for the smallest extremes as mentioned by Barnett and de Peretti (2009). For more information related to the extreme value distributions for the extremes, see Guégan (2003), Hosking, Wallis, and Wood (1985), and Rootzén (1986).

our Gaussian assumption about the model's innovations, the two extremes reside in the domain of attraction of the type I Gumbel law [see, e.g., Barnett and de Peretti (2009)]. Therefore, testing the significance of the violation of GARP is achieved by computing the two p-values for the maxima and the minima, respectively:

$$1 - exp\left\{-exp\left[-(\widehat{Max_j} - a_{1j})b_{1j}^{-1}\right]\right\} \quad (3.6)$$

$$1 - exp\left\{-exp\left[-(\widehat{Min_j} - a_{2j})b_{2j}^{-1}\right]\right\} \quad (3.7)$$

where a_{1j} and a_{2j} denote location parameters for the maximum and the minimum of the measurement error $\boldsymbol{\psi}_{.j}$ with corresponding scale parameters b_{1j} and b_{2j}. However, the values of the location and scale parameters are unknowns, because the true measurement error Ψ is not observable, and hence has to be estimated.

To overcome this problem, Barnett and de Peretti (2009) considered the state-space representation of the model. In particular, model (3.3) denotes the measurement equation in a state-space model. To complete the transition equation, we must specify the process for the unobserved variable. In line with Barnett and de Peretti (2009), we assume a random walk process without drift for our unobservable variable along with the normality of the model's innovations. Mathematically, our state-space representatins for good j takes the following form:

$$x_{ij} = x_{ij}^* + \psi_{ij} \quad (3.8)$$

$$x_{(i+1)j}^* = \mathrm{x}_{\mathrm{ij}}^* + \zeta_{\mathrm{ij}} \quad (3.9)$$

where $\psi_{ij} \sim N(0, \sigma_{\psi_j}^2)$ and $\zeta_{ij} \sim N(0, \sigma_{\zeta_j}^2)$ are uncorrelated residuals. Equations (3.8) and (3.9) are known as the measurement and transition equations, respectively. To proceed, we perform the following simulation procedure proposed by Stoffer and Wall (1991). For good $j, j = 1, \ldots, k,$ define $x_{ij|T}^*$ as the smoothed estimate of the unobserved variable x_{ij}^* computed by Kalman filter and let

$\widehat{\boldsymbol{\psi}_{.j}} = (\hat{\psi}_{1j}, \hat{\psi}_{2j}, ..., \hat{\psi}_{Tj})$ be the corresponding smoothed residuals where $\hat{\psi}_{ij} = x_{ij} - x^{*}_{ij|T}, i = 1, ..., T.$ Let $\widehat{Max_{\psi_j}} = max(\hat{\psi}_{1j}, \hat{\psi}_{2j}, ..., \hat{\psi}_{Tj})$ and $\widehat{Min_{\psi_j}} = min(\hat{\psi}_{1j}, \hat{\psi}_{2j}, ..., \hat{\psi}_{Tj})$. Define $x^{*}_{(i+1)j|i}$ as the best linear predictor of $x^{*}_{(i+1)j}$ obtained via Kalman filter. Consider the following innovation representation form of the Kalman filter:

$$x_{ij} = x^{*}_{ij|i-1} + \varepsilon_{ij} \tag{3.10}$$

$$x^{*}_{(i+1)j|i} = x^{*}_{ij|i-1} + K_{ij}\varepsilon_{ij} \tag{3.11}$$

where $\varepsilon_{ij} = x_{ij} - x^{*}_{ij|i-1}$ is the innovation, $K_{ij} = P_{ij|i-1}\Sigma^{-1}_{ij}$ is the Kalman gain within which $P_{ij|i-1}$ is the covariance matrix of $x^{*}_{ij} - x^{*}_{ij|i-1}$ and $\Sigma_{ij} = P_{ij|i-1} + \sigma^{2}_{\psi_j}$.

Denote $\boldsymbol{\theta}$ as the stacked vector of hyperparametes estimated by maximum likelihood. The Monte Carlo bootstrap procedure consists of the following steps:[11]

Step1: Compute the standardized residual:

$$\upsilon_{ij}(\boldsymbol{\theta}) = \Sigma^{-1/2}_{ij}(\boldsymbol{\theta})\varepsilon_{ij}(\boldsymbol{\theta})$$

Step2: Sample the standardized residual $\upsilon_{ij}(\boldsymbol{\theta})$, with replacement, T times. This will generate a bootstrap sample of standardized residuals, $\{\upsilon^{s}_{ij}(\boldsymbol{\theta})\}^{T}_{i=1}$.

Step3: In equation (3.11), substitute ε_{ij} with $\Sigma^{1/2}_{ij}(\boldsymbol{\theta})\upsilon^{s}_{ij}(\boldsymbol{\theta})$ to obtain a bootstrap series $x^{*s}_{(i+1)j|i}(\boldsymbol{\theta})$. In equation (3.10), replace ε_{ij} by $\Sigma^{1/2}_{ij}(\boldsymbol{\theta})\upsilon^{s}_{ij}(\boldsymbol{\theta})$ and (while maintaining the same initial conditions) use $x^{*s}_{(i+1)j|i}(\boldsymbol{\theta})$ to

[11] See Stoffer and Wall (1991) for a more complete discussion and see Barnett and de Peretti (2009) for more clarifications.

acquire new bootstrap series x_{ij}^{s}.

Step4: Once the bootstrap series x_{ij}^{s} is generated, we re-estimate the model and compute the maximum and the minimum of $\widehat{\psi}_{.j}$.

We repeat the procedure 1000 times and we store the maximums and the minimums of the smoothed residuals $\widehat{\psi}_{.j}$. This procedure returns two series of bootstrap maximums and minimums [Barnett and de Peretti (2009)]. The scale and location parameters of the Gumbal law are then computed by simply using the moments method.[12]

As a robustness test, we also apply the method proposed by Guégan (2003) to compute the scale and location parameters. Specifically, under our Gaussian assumptions, Guégan (2003) has shown that the maximum of a series of T variates drawn in a centered and reduced normal law has (3.6) as a limiting distribution with the following location and scale parameters, respectively:

$$\gamma_j = \sqrt{2ln(T)} - \left\{ \frac{ln\left[ln(T)\right] + ln(4\pi)}{2\sqrt{2ln(T)}} \right\} \tag{3.12}$$

$$\eta_j = \left[2ln(T)\right]^{-1/2} \tag{3.13}$$

Define $\widehat{Max}_{R_j} = max\left(\widehat{\omega}_{1j}\widehat{\sigma}_{\psi_j}^{-1}, \widehat{\omega}_{2j}\widehat{\sigma}_{\psi_j}^{-1}, \ldots, \widehat{\omega}_{Tj}\widehat{\sigma}_{\psi_j}^{-1}\right)$ and $\widehat{Min}_{R_j} = min\left(\widehat{\omega}_{1j}\widehat{\sigma}_{\psi_j}^{-1}, \widehat{\omega}_{2j}\widehat{\sigma}_{\psi_j}^{-1}, \ldots, \widehat{\omega}_{Tj}\widehat{\sigma}_{\psi_j}^{-1}\right)$, where $\hat{\sigma}_{\psi_j}$ is the maximum likelihood estimate of σ_{ψ_j}. Hence, testing the significance of the adjustments for good j is achieved by computing the p-values for the maxima and the minima respectively:

---

[12] Other methods of calculating the scale and location parameters include the maximum likelihood and the probability weighted moments. See Barnett and de Peretti (2009) for more details.

$$1 - exp\left\{-exp\left[-\left(\widehat{Max}_{R_j} - \gamma_j\right)\eta_j^{-1}\right]\right\} \tag{3.14}$$

$$1 - exp\left\{-exp\left[-\left(\widehat{Min}_{R_j} - \widetilde{\gamma}_j\right)\eta_j^{-1}\right]\right\} \tag{3.15}$$

where $\widetilde{\gamma}_j = -\gamma_j$.

If the violations are found to be significant, then one can conclude that there is no weak separability in the utility function. On the other hand, if the violations are nonsignificant and hence caused by purely stochastic factors such as measurement errors, we then test for weak separability.

It is obvious that condition (iii) can be misleading since the indexes U_i produce an ordinal measurement rather than cardinal measurement and hence remains only sufficient condition [de Peretti (2005)]. To remedy this problem, Barnett and de Peretti (2009) substituted condition (iii) with one that is derived from the microeconomic concept "Marginal Rate of Substitution" which is indeed a necessary and sufficient condition. Specifically, weak separability implies that the marginal rate of substitution between goods within a separable group is independent of goods outside the group [Deaton and Muellbauer (1980)]:

$$\frac{\partial\left(\dfrac{\partial U(\mathbf{x}_{\mathrm{i}}) / \partial \mathrm{x}_{\mathrm{ij}}}{\partial U(\mathbf{x}_{\mathrm{i}}) / \partial x_{il}}\right)}{\partial x_{im}} = \frac{\partial\left(\dfrac{p_{ij}}{p_{il}}\right)}{\partial x_{im}} = 0 \tag{3.16}$$

for $j,l = 1,...,a; j \neq l; m = a+1,...,k$ and $i = 1,...,T$.

At the optimum, marginal rate of substitution between goods equals their relative prices. This has a significant implication on the way of testing weak separability manifested in the fact that knowing the functional form of the utility function is not necessary because prices are observable. Therefore, testing the weak separability of a group of assets is straightforward. If all unique price ratios of within group assets are independent from outside quantities, then the inside group assets are said to be weakly separable.

Let $r = \sum_{i=1}^{a-1}(a-i)$ where $a \in \{1,...,k-1\}$. Define $\mathbf{Y}$ as a $(T \cdot r \times 1)$ vector of all unique ratios of user costs pertaining to monetary assets within a weakly separable monetary aggregate. In a matrix form,

$$\mathbf{Y} = \begin{bmatrix} log\ (\boldsymbol{\pi}_{.1}/\boldsymbol{\pi}_{.2}) \\ log\ (\boldsymbol{\pi}_{.1}/\boldsymbol{\pi}_{.3}) \\ \vdots \\ log\ (\boldsymbol{\pi}_{.1}/\boldsymbol{\pi}_{.a}) \\ log\ (\boldsymbol{\pi}_{.2}/\boldsymbol{\pi}_{.3}) \\ \vdots \\ log\ (\boldsymbol{\pi}_{.2}/\boldsymbol{\pi}_{.a}) \\ \vdots \\ log\ (\boldsymbol{\pi}_{.(a-1)}/\boldsymbol{\pi}_{.a}) \end{bmatrix}$$

where $\boldsymbol{\pi}_{.j} = (\pi_{1j}, \pi_{2j}, \dots, \pi_{Tj})$ denotes the jth $(j = 1, \dots, a)$ column of $\boldsymbol{\Pi}$. Similarly, let $\mathbf{W} = [\mathbf{1} \;\; log(\mathbf{X}^*)] = [\mathbf{1} \;\; log(\mathbf{M}^*) \;\; log(\mathbf{C}^*)]$ be a $(T \times (k+1))$ matrix. Our model is written in the following form:

$$\mathbf{Y} = \begin{bmatrix} \mathbf{W} & 0 & \cdots & 0 \\ 0 & \mathbf{W} & & \vdots \\ \vdots & \vdots & \ddots & \\ 0 & 0 & \cdots & \mathbf{W} \end{bmatrix} \begin{bmatrix} \boldsymbol{\beta}_1 \\ \boldsymbol{\beta}_2 \\ \vdots \\ \boldsymbol{\beta}_r \end{bmatrix} + \epsilon \qquad (3.17)$$

where, for $i = 1, \dots, r$; $\boldsymbol{\beta}_i = [\boldsymbol{\beta}_i^{o} \;\; \boldsymbol{\beta}_i^{m} \;\; \boldsymbol{\beta}_i^{c}]$ is a $((k+1)\times 1)$ parameter vector. Under the null, the monetary aggregates are weakly separable from private consumption. Empirically, testing the weak separability of the monetary aggregates is equivalent to testing the nullity of the consumption's parameters such that:

$$(iv) \qquad \boldsymbol{\beta}_1^c = \boldsymbol{\beta}_2^c = \cdots = \boldsymbol{\beta}_r^c = \mathbf{0}$$

We use condition (iv) instead of condition (iii) for testing the weak separability. Specifically, the weak separability of the monetary aggregate, $\mathbf{M}^*$, from private consumption, $\mathbf{C}^*$, is achieved when $\boldsymbol{\beta}_i^c = \mathbf{0}$, for $i = 1, \dots, r$. This implies that the marginal rate of substitution between monetary assets within a monetary aggregate (inside group assets) is independent from the outside goods. It is worthwhile to mention that whenever violations of GARP are nonsignificant, we estimate model (3.17) by using the smoothed estimates of the state vector computed by Kalman filter as suggested by Barnett and de Peretti (2009).

3.3 Data

3.3.1 Data Descriptions and Sources

The analysis in this study is based on monthly data starting as far back as the data were available and ending in December 2011. Consumer Price Indexes (CPI), interest rates, and other monetary data were obtained from the GCC central banks, International Financial Statistics, Federal Reserve Economic Data, Bloomberg database, and the GCC Secretariat General. The monetary assets for the Gulf countries include currency in circulation, overnight deposits, demand deposits, saving and time deposits, and quasi-money. The benchmark rates as well as the user costs for all monetary assets were obtained from Alkhareif and Barnett (2012).

The paper also uses data on consumption of durable and non-durable goods and their corresponding prices from the GCC central banks and the U.S. Energy Information Administration. Since the consumption data were only available in annual series, we interpolated the annual consumption of durables and non-durables using relevant monthly data such as the imports of durable and non-durable goods. In particular, we implemented the state-space model for interpolation introduced by Stock and Watson (2010). Using related prices and population data for the GCC countries, we convert the total private consumption and monetary assets to real per capita terms. Finally, all quantities have been seasonally adjusted using the $X11$ procedure and converted to U.S. dollar values.

3.3.2 Divisia Aggregation of the Gulf Consumption

This section describes the methodology of constructing the GCC area consumption. We use the microeconomic aggregation and index number theory developed by Barnett (1980a,b; 1987; 2003; and 2007) to aggregate consumption over the GCC countries. Mathematically, we proceed as follows. Let K be the number of countries in the Gulf monetary union. For each country $k \in \{1,...,K\}$, define the true cost-of-living index as $p_k^* = p_k^*(\mathbf{p}_k)$, where $\mathbf{p}_k = \mathbf{p}_k(t)$ represents the vector of prices of consumer goods at time t. Let

C_k be the within-country, consumer-goods, per-capita aggregates.

e_k be country $k's$ currency exchange rate against a market basket of currencies.

$s_k = \frac{H_k}{\Sigma_{k=1}^{K} H_k}$ be country $k's$ share of total GCC population, where H_k denotes country $k's$ population.

Define country $k's$ expenditure share of the Gulf consumption by:

$$B_k = \frac{C_k p_k^* e_k}{\Sigma_{k=1}^{K} C_k p_k^* e_k}$$

where $0 \leq B_k \leq 1$ and $\Sigma_{k=1}^{K} B_k = 1$.

Definition 1: The Divisia indexes for the Gulf area's nominal and real per-capita consumption aggregates respectively are defined as:

$$\frac{dlogC}{dt} = \Sigma_{k=1}^{K} B_k \frac{dlog(C_k s_k e_k)}{dt} \qquad (3.18)$$

$$\frac{dlogC^*}{dt} = \Sigma_{k=1}^{K} B_k \frac{dlog(C_k^* s_k)}{dt} \qquad (3.19)$$

The corresponding discrete time representation of the continues time Divisia indexes (3.18) and (3.19) are:

$$logC_t - logC_{t-1} = \Sigma_{k=1}^{K} B_{kt}^* \left[log(C_{kt} s_{kt} e_{kt}) - log(C_{k,t-1} s_{k,t-1} e_{k,t-1}) \right]$$

$$logC_t^* - logC_{t-1}^* = \Sigma_{k=1}^{K} B_{kt}^* \left[log(C_{kt}^* s_{kt}) - log(C_{k,t-1}^* s_{k,t-1}) \right]$$

where $B_{kt}^* = (1/2)\left(B_{kt} + B_{k,t-1}\right)$

In levels, the nominal and real Divisia consumption aggregates, respectively, are:

$$\frac{C_t}{C_{t-1}} = \Pi_{k=1}^{K} \left(\frac{C_{kt} s_{kt} e_{kt}}{C_{k,t-1} s_{k,t-1} e_{k,t-1}} \right)^{B_{kt}^*}$$

$$\frac{C_t^*}{C_{t-1}^*} = \Pi_{k=1}^{K}\left(\frac{C_{kt}^* s_{kt}}{C_{k,t-1}^* s_{k,t-1}}\right)^{B_{kt}^*}$$

3.4 Testing for the Existence of the GCC Common Currency Area

We consider two groupings of monetary assets. The first group includes all monetary assets available in the economy. For the GCC countries, the group consists of currency in circulation, demand deposits, quasi-money, savings and time deposits. The second group is a subset of the first group where only currency in circulations and demand deposits are included. Our choice of these groupings was not arbitrary, but rather was designed to foster the Gulf monetary council's effort to maintain a common currency area. Specifically, we exam the weak separability of the current monetary aggregates for the GCC countries. First, we test the weak separability of all monetary assets within the broad monetary aggregate (i.e., currency in circulations, demand deposits, quasi-money, savings and time deposits) from private consumption. If the data pass the weak separability test then we have accomplished the weak separability thereby the existence of the broad monetary aggregate $M2$. Once weak separability of all monetary assets is established, we then test the weak separability of the liquid monetary assets (i.e., currency in circulation, demand deposits) from the others. Weak separability of these liquid assets implies the existence of the narrowed monetary aggregate, namely $M1$.

Our goal is to first test the weak separability of the narrow and broad monetary aggregates for each country individually. We begin by testing monetary components and private consumption along with their associated prices for GARP. Our results indicate that data sets for the sub-utility as well as the overall utility for most countries have passed GARP test without violations, except for Kuwait (Table 3-1). The GARP test for the broad monetary aggregate in Kuwait reports violations for the sub-utility function. These violations are likely driven by the fact that Kuwait, unlike other GCC countries, pegs its currency to a basket of currencies rather than maintaining a fixed exchange rate. Nonetheless, all of the violations are due to stochastic or measurement errors thereby they are nonsignificant (Table 3-1). Therefore, we conclude that our data sets satisfy GARP—for both the sub-utility as well as the overall utility.

Our findings suggest that components in the broad monetary aggregate, $M2$, for all GCC countries are weakly separable from consumption

(Table 3-1). For condition (iv), we fail to reject the null of weak separability for all countries except Qatar. While the broad monetary aggregates exist for Qatar, the narrow one does not exist. Our results indicate that demand deposits cannot be clustered with currency in circulations given the interest rate nature of the former (Table 3-2). Unlike the rest of Gulf countries, demand deposits in Qatar offer positive interest rates and hence the one-to-one substitutability between currency and demand deposits no longer hold. As a result, currency in circulation will be the only asset in the narrow monetary aggregate in Qatar. This will lead to zero violations for GARP tests as well as the existence of both monetary aggregates $M1$ and $M2$.

For the GCC union, GARP test is performed on all of the GCC monetary assets to test the admissibility of clustering them into one single currency. Our results are in line with the ones in Fleissig and Whitney (2008), in which the violations for GARP are due to measurement errors and hence are nonsignificant. As shown in Table 3-1, all of the violations are resulted from some stochastic and measurement errors which are nonsignificant. Thus, we procced to check for condition *(iv)*.

The broad monetary aggregate for the GCC union, $M2$, satisfies condition (iv) implying the existence of a monetary aggregator function over all monetary assets in the Gulf area (Table 3-1). However, monetary assets within $M1$ (currency in circulations and demand deposits) failed condition (iv) and hence the narrow monetary aggregate for the GCC union does not exist (Table 3-2). We find that demand deposits in Qatar cannot be clustered with Gulf currency, but rather clustered with short term deposits (e.g., quasi-money, savings and time deposits). This is due to the fact that demand deposits in Qatar offer positive interest rates just like other Gulf short-term deposits. In addition, currency in circulation and demand deposits in Oman are heterogeneous with respect to other GCC countries in the sense that they do not form a monetary aggregate with the rest of the countries' monetary assets (Table 3-2). This could be attributed to the fact that Oman is a non-oil producing country and hence the Omani economic structure differs from its GCC counterparts. Since Oman is not an oil dependent country as opposed to the others, it is more likely that Oman will experience different external shocks making the monetary assets behave differently than they do in the oil dependent countries.

To remedy this problem, we proposed alternative groupings of the GCC area monetary assets where we exclude Oman from the monetary union. In addition, the demand deposits in Qatar (which offer positive interest rates) are excluded from the narrow monetary aggregate M1.

Therefore, the narrow monetary aggregate for the GCC union, $M1$, will be an aggregate of only monetary assets that bear zero-interest rates. In contrast, the broad monetary aggregate for the GCC union will encompass the components in $M1$ as well as less liquid assets that offer some positive rate of return. As indicated in Tables 3-1 and 3-2, the GARP violations for the overall GCC union remain nonsignificant. This result indicates that violations are due to stochastic or other measurement errors. For condition (iv), we fail to reject the null of weak separability for both the narrow aggregate as well as the broad aggregate. Consequently, the overall findings indicate the existence of both $M1$ and $M2$ monetary aggregates for the GCC union.

3.5 Constructing Divisia Monetary Aggregates for Admissible Groupings of the GCC Area

In the previous section, we provided admissible groupings of monetary assets for individual GCC countries and then for the GCC area that are weakly separable. Based upon these admissible groups of monetary assets, we construct Divisia monetary aggregates for the GCC countries and then build a single Divisia index for the GCC area. The GCC admissible monetary aggregates $M1$ and $M2$ are computed using two approaches of aggregation: i) the first approach is the traditional simple-sum monetary aggregation, which is used by many central banks worldwide ii) the second approach is known as the Divisia monetary aggregation which is based upon microeconomic theory and index number theory.[13] We compare our Divisia monetary aggregates to the officially published simple-sum monetary aggregates.[14] The simple-sum monetary aggregates are computed by simply summing up monetary assets all with unity share weights (i.e., it implicitly assumes perfect substitutability among monetary assets).

---

[13] Divisia index belongs to the class of superlative index numbers defined by Diewet (1976). Moreover, Divisia index is exact for the quadratic translog specification of the exact aggregator function. See Barnett (1982) for a more complete discussion.

[14] Barnett (2012) provides a comparison analysis between major monetary indexes including the Divisia and simple-sum indexes. In addition, the Center for Financial Stability (CFS) in New York City provides a directory on the literature pertaining to Divisia monetary aggregations for over 40 countries throughout the world. For more information on Divisia monetary aggregates, visit the CFS website at www.centerforfinancialstability.org/amfm.php.

We begin constructing the GCC area Divisia monetary aggregates by using those admissible groupings of monetary assets across GCC countries. Specifically, the construction of Divisia monetary aggregates for the Gulf area is recursively computed in two stages. In the first stage, Divisia quantity and price indexes are computed for all individual countries. Since each country has its own benchmark rate, user costs of monetary assets will vary across countries even if these assets provide the same rate of return. In the second stage, we construct the Divisia monetary aggregates for the Gulf area by using the Divisia quantity and price indexes found in stage 1. We use the theory provided by Theil (1967) and Barnett (1979a; 1979b; 1980b) and extended in Barnett (2003, 2007) to multilateral aggregation permitting aggregation within and then over countries.[15] To circumvent redundancy, this paper only reports the definitions for the relevant Divisia indexes and we refer to Barnett (2003, 2007) and Alkhareif and Barnett (2012) for a more complete discussion.

Stage 1. Constructing Divisia quantity and price aggregates for the GCC countries

We are interested in calculating the Divisia quantity and price indexes for each country. As a preliminary step, we compute the prices (user costs) of all monetary assets taken into consideration when constructing the Divisia indexes. User cost is a key concept in aggregation and index number theory. User cost is defined as the interest return forgone by holding a monetary asset rather than holding asset(s) with maximum returns [Barnett (1978)]. Barnett (2003, 2007) defined the real user-cost price of asset i purchased in country j and owned by economic agent(s) living in country k at time t as:[16]

$$\pi_{kji}^{*}(t) = R_k(t) - r_{kji}(t),$$

where

$R_k(t) = R_k$ is country $k's$ benchmark rate at time t.[17]

---

[15] A complete discussion regarding the Divisia monetary aggregates for the GCC countries is provided by Alkhareif and Barnett (2012).

[16] The real and nominal user cost prices are related to one another by the following direct relationship: $\pi_{kji}(t) = p_k^{*}(t)\pi_{kji}^{*}(t)$, where $p_k^{*}(t)$ denotes country $k's$ true cost–of–living index at time t.

[17] Barnett (1987) defined the benchmark rate to be the yield on a pure investment

$r_{kji}(t) = r_{kji}$ is the rate of return on asset i purchased in country j and owned by economic agent(s) of country k at time t.

Definition 2 [Barnett (2007)]: For each GCC country, $k \in \{1,...,K\}$, let

$$w_{kji} = \frac{\pi_{kji} m^*_{kji}}{\boldsymbol{\pi}_k' \mathbf{m}^*_k} = \frac{\pi^*_{kji} m^*_{kji}}{\boldsymbol{\pi}^{*\prime}_k \mathbf{m}^*_k} = \frac{(R_k - r_{kji}) m^*_{kji}}{\sum_{(j,i)\in S_k} (R_k - r_{kji}) m^*_{kji}} = \frac{(R_k - r_{kji}) m_{kji}}{\sum_{(j,i)\in S_k} (R_k - r_{kji}) m_{kji}}.$$

The discrete time representation of the real per-capita monetary services aggregate M^*_k, the nominal per-capita monetary services aggregate M_k, the real user-cost price aggregate Π^*_k, and the nominal user-cost price aggregate Π_k, respectively are:[18]

$$\log M^*_{kt} - \log M^*_{k,t-1} = \sum_{(j,i)\in S_k} w^*_{kjit} \left(\log m^*_{kjit} - \log m^*_{kji,t-1} \right)$$

$$\log M_{kt} - \log M_{k,t-1} = \sum_{(j,i)\in S_k} w^*_{kjit} \left(\log m_{kjit} - \log m_{kji,t-1} \right)$$

$$\log \Pi^*_{kt} - \log \Pi^*_{k,t-1} = \sum_{(j,i)\in S_k} w^*_{kjit} \left(\log \pi^*_{kjit} - \log \pi^*_{kji,t-1} \right)$$

$$\log \Pi_{kt} - \log \Pi_{k,t-1} = \sum_{(j,i)\in S_k} w^*_{kjit} \left(\log \pi_{kjit} - \log \pi_{kji,t-1} \right)$$

where $w^*_{kjit} = (1/2)\left(w_{kjit} + w_{kji,t-1} \right)$.

---

asset, held solely to accumulate wealth and providing no other services, such as liquidity. See Barnett (2012) and Alkhareif and Barnett (2012) for further details pertaining to the benchmark rate.

[18] Barnett (2003, 2007) and Alkhareif and Barnett (2012) provide the continues time representation of the Divisia quantity and price indexes.

Stage 2. Constructing Divisia monetary aggregates over the Gulf area

Given that we acquired the Divisia quantity and price indexes for individual countries, constructing the Divisia monetary aggregates for the GCC area is now straightforward. For each GCC country, $k \in \{1,...,K\}$, define country $k's$ expenditure share of the Gulf union's monetary service flow as:

$$W_k = \frac{M_k^* \Pi_k^* p_k^* e_k s_k}{\sum_{k=1}^{K} M_k^* \Pi_k^* p_k^* e_k s_k} = \frac{M_k \Pi_k^* e_k s_k}{\sum_{k=1}^{K} M_k \Pi_k^* e_k s_k} = \frac{M_k^* \Pi_k e_k s_k}{\sum_{k=1}^{K} M_k^* \Pi_k e_k s_k},$$

where $0 \leq W_k \leq 1$ and $\sum_{k=1}^{K} W_k = 1$.

Definition 3 [Barnett (2007)]: The growth rates of the Gulf area's real and nominal per-capita monetary service flows respectively are:

$$\log M_t^* - \log M_{t-1}^* = \sum_{k=1}^{K} W_{kt}^* \;(\log M_{kt}^* s_{kt} - \log M_{k,t-1}^* s_{k,t-1}) \tag{3.20}$$

$$\log M_t - \log M_{t-1} = \sum_{k=1}^{K} W_{kt}^* (\log M_{kt} s_{kt} e_{kt} - \log M_{k,t-1} s_{k,t-1} e_{k,t-1}) \tag{3.21}$$

where $W_{kt}^* = (1/2)(W_{kt} + W_{k,t-1})$.

Figure 3-1 depicts the year-over-year growth rates of the Divisia and simple-sum narrow monetary aggregates. Our findings are in line with those of Alkhareif and Barnett (2012) in which the two approaches of aggregation produce identical results for the narrow monetary aggregate $M1$. The reason behind the equivalence between the narrow Divisia and simple-sum monetary aggregates is twofold: first, all monetary assets within $M1$ bear zero-interest rates, and hence similar in nature; second, the benchmark rates for the GCC countries are relatively the same. On the other hand, the two approaches to aggregations reveal a clear distinction for the broad monetary aggregate $M2$ (Figure 3-2). The variations between the growth rates of Divisia and simple-sum broad monetary aggregates are likely driven by variations in the user costs of monetary assets within the Gulf area's broad monetary aggregate $M2$. The long run growth rates of Divisia monetary aggregates exemplify the business cycles, during which the growth rates are high in the economic boom—fueled by large oil revenues and massive government spending on infrastructure projects—and low afterwards, in periods when oil prices dropped sharply as a consequence of the distress over the global economy [Alkhareif and Barnett (2012)]. Figures 3-1 and 3-2 suggest that the narrow aggregates grew while broad aggregates collapsed following the financial crises—implying the potential disability of the financial system in the GCC area to create liquidity during the crises [Alkhareif and Barnett (2012)].

3.5 Conclusion

Using the semi-nonparametric test for weak separability proposed by Barnett and de Peretti (2009), this paper investigates the weak separability of the currently defined monetary aggregates $M1$ and $M2$ for the GCC countries. Our results indicate weak separability thereby the existence of the monetary aggregates $M1$ and $M2$ for each GCC countries except Qatar. The narrow monetary aggregate, $M1$, for Qatar failed to pass the weak separability test. In particular, demand deposits, which offer positive interest rate, cannot be clustered with currency in circulation —which yields zero interest. Thus, we propose a new narrow monetary aggregate $M1$ that comprises only the currency in circulation, an aggregate that is weakly separable.

After constructing admissible monetary aggregates $M1$ and $M2$ for all GCC countries, we test the weak separability of monetary assets across countries. Our findings imply the existence of the GCC area broad monetary aggregate $M2$, but not $M1$. We find that liquid assets (i.e. currency in circulation and demand deposits) in Oman cannot be grouped with the ones for other GCC countries. Both monetary aggregates $M1$ and $M2$ for the GCC area exist once we exclude Oman. Thus, the remaining countries form a common currency area.

Using our admissible groups of monetary assets, we construct Divisia and simple-sum monetary aggregates for the GCC area. When constructing the Divisia indexes, we follow the multilateral aggregation approach found in Barnett (2003, 2007) and Alkhareif and Barnett (2012). In particular, we construct Divisia monetary aggregates for the GCC area recursively by first building the Divisia monetary indexes for the GCC countries and then aggregate across countries. Our findings indicate Divisia monetary growth rates are low prior to recessions, while those growth rates increase at a faster pace than simple-sum during recoveries [Alkhareif and Barnett (2012)]. Moreover, the gap between Divisia and simple-sum growth rates widened during times of high uncertainty and periods of economic disruptions, such as the financial turmoil. We conclude that Divisia indexes perform better in monitoring the business cycles that is consistent with GCC monetary policy.

References

Alkhareif, R. M. , and Barnett, W. A. (2012). Divisia Monetary Aggregates for the GCC Countries. *In William A. Barnett and Fredj Jawadi (eds.), Recent Developments in Alternative Finance: Empirical Assessments and Economic Implications (International Symposia in Economic Theory and Econometrics, (Vol.22), Emerald Group Publishing Limited*, pp.1-37.

Barnett, W. A. (1978). The user cost of money. *Economics Letters, 1*(2), 145-149.

—. (1979a). The Joint Allocation of Leisure and Goods Expenditure. *Econometrica, 47*(3), 539-563.

—. (1979b). Theoretical Foundations for the Rotterdam Model. *Review of Economic Studies, 46*(1), 109-130.

—. (1980a). Economic monetary aggregates--reply. *Journal of Econometrics, 14*(1), 57-59.

—. (1980b). Economic monetary aggregates an application of index number and aggregation theory. *Journal of Econometrics, 14*(1), 11-48.

—. (1982). The Optimal Level of Monetary Aggregation. *Journal of Money, Credit and Banking, 14*(4), 687-710.

—. (1987). The Microeconomic Theory of Monetary Aggregation. *New Approaches to Monetary Economics,* Cambridge U. Press.

—. (2003). Aggregation-Theoretic Monetary Aggregation over the Euro Area, when Countries are Heterogeneous: *EconWPA*.

—. (2007). Multilateral aggregation-theoretic monetary aggregation over heterogeneous countries. *Journal of Econometrics, 136*(2), 457-482.

—. (2012). Getting it wrong : how faulty monetary statistics undermine the Fed, the financial system, and the economy. MIT Press, Boston.

Barnett, W. A., and Choi, S. (1989). A Monte Carlo Study of Tests of Blockwise Weak Separability. *Journal of Business and Economic Statistics, 7*(3), 363-377.

Barnett, W. A., and de Peretti, P. (2009). Admissible Clustering Of Aggregator Components: A Necessary And Sufficient Stochastic Seminonparametric Test For Weak Separability. *Macroeconomic Dynamics, 13*(52), 317-334.

Binner, J. M., Bissoondeeal, R. K., Elger, C. T., Jones, B. E., and Mullineux, A. W. (2009). Admissible monetary aggregates for the euro area. *Journal of International Money and Finance, 28*(1), 99-114.

de Peretti, P. (2005). Testing The Significance Of The Departures From Utility Maximization. *Macroeconomic Dynamics, 9*(03), 372-397.

—. (2007). Testing the Significance of the Departures from Weak Separability. *International Symposia in Economic Theory and Econometrics: Functional Structure Inference, William Barnett and Apostolos Serletis, Eds. Elsevier Press.*

Deaton, A., and Muellbauer, J. (1980). Economics and Consumer Behavior. Cambridge University Press.

Diewert, W. E. (1976). Exact and superlative index numbers. *Journal of Econometrics, 4*(2), 115-145.

Fleissig, A. R., and Whitney, G. A. (2003). A New PC-Based Test for Varian's Weak Separability Conditions. *Journal of Business and Economic Statistics, 21*(1), 133-144.

Fleissig, A. R., and Whitney, G. A. (2005). Testing for the Significance of Violations of Afriat's Inequalities. *Journal of Business and Economic Statistics, 23*(3), 355-362.

Fleissig, A. R., and Whitney, G. A. (2008). A nonparametric test of weak separability and consumer preferences. *Journal of Econometrics, 147*(2), 275-281.

Guégan, D. (2003). Introduction aux Valeurs extrémes et à ses Applications. *Working paper., Ecole Normale Supérieure de Cachan.*

Hosking, J. R. M., Wallis, J. R., and Wood, E. F. (1985). Estimation of the Generalized Extreme-Value Distribution by the Method of Probability-Weighted Moments. *Technometrics, 27*(3), 251-261.

Kenen, P. B. (1969). The Theory of Optimum Currency Areas. In *e. R. A. Mundell and A. K. Swoboda (Ed.), Monetary Problems of the International Economy* (pp. 41-60). *Chicago*: Chicago University Press.

McKinnon, R. I. (1963). Optimum Currency Areas. *The American Economic Review, 53*(4), 717-725.

Mundell, R. A. (1961). A Theory of Optimum Currency Areas. *The American Economic Review, 51*(4), 657-665.

Rootzén, H. (1986). Extreme Value Theory for Moving Average Processes. *The Annals of Probability, 14*(2), 612-652.

Serletis, A. (2001). The Demand for Money: Theoretical and Empirical

Approaches. *Kluwer Academic Publishers*.
Stock, J. H., and Watson, M. W. (2010). Distribution of quarterly values of GDP/GDI across months within the quarter. Department of Economics and Woodrow Wilson School, *Research Memorandum.*
Stoffer, D. S., and Wall, K. D. (1991). Bootstrapping State-Space Models: Gaussian Maximum Likelihood Estimation and the Kalman Filter. *Journal of the American Statistical Association, 86*(416), 1024-1033.
Swofford, J. L. (2000). Microeconomic foundations of an optimal currency area. *Review of Financial Economics, 9*(2), 121-128.
Swofford, J. L., and Whitney, G. A. (1987). Nonparametric Tests of Utility Maximization and Weak Separability for Consumption, Leisure and Money. *The Review of Economics and Statistics, 69*(3), 458-464.
Swofford, J. L., and Whitney, G. A. (1994). A revealed preference test for weakly separable utility maximization with incomplete adjustment. *Journal of Econometrics, 60*(1-2), 235-249.
Theil, H. (1967). *Economics and information theory*. Elsevier, Amsterdam.
Varian, H. R. (1982). The Nonparametric Approach to Demand Analysis. *Econometrica, 50*(4), 945-973.
—. (1983). Non-Parametric Tests of Consumer Behaviour. *Review of Economic Studies, 50*(1), 99-110.
—. (1985). Non-parametric analysis of optimizing behavior with measurement error. *Journal of Econometrics, 30*(1-2), 445-458.

Table 3-1: Weak Separability of M2 from Private Consumption

Country	GARP Violations		Weak Separability Test	
	Sub-utility	Overall utility	P-value	Weak separability
Bahrain	0	0	0.12	Y
Kuwait	302	0	0.69	Y
Oman	0	0	0.86	Y
Qatar	0	0	0.74	Y
KSA	0	0	0.69	Y
UAE	0	0	0.96	Y
GCC Area I	13	0	0.52	Y
GCC Area II	4	0	0.46	Y

Notes: All violations of GARP are not statistically significant at 90% confidence level. The "GCC Area I" comprises all GCC countries whereas "GCC Area II" excludes Oman.

Table 3-2: Weak Separability of M1 from M2

Country	GARP Violations		Weak Separability Test	
	Sub-utility	Overall utility	P-value	Weak separability
Bahrain	0	0	1	Y
Kuwait	0	0	1	Y
Oman	0	0	1	Y
Qatar	0	0	0	N
KSA	0	0	1	Y
UAE	0	0	1	Y
GCC Area I	4	13	0	N
GCC Area II	0	4	0.41	Y

Notes: All violations of GARP are not statistically significant at 90% confidence level. The "GCC Area I" comprises all GCC countries whereas "GCC Area II" excludes Oman.

Figure 3-1: Year-Over-Year Growth Rates of the Divisia and Simple-Sum Monetary Aggregates, M1 (Annual Percentage Change)

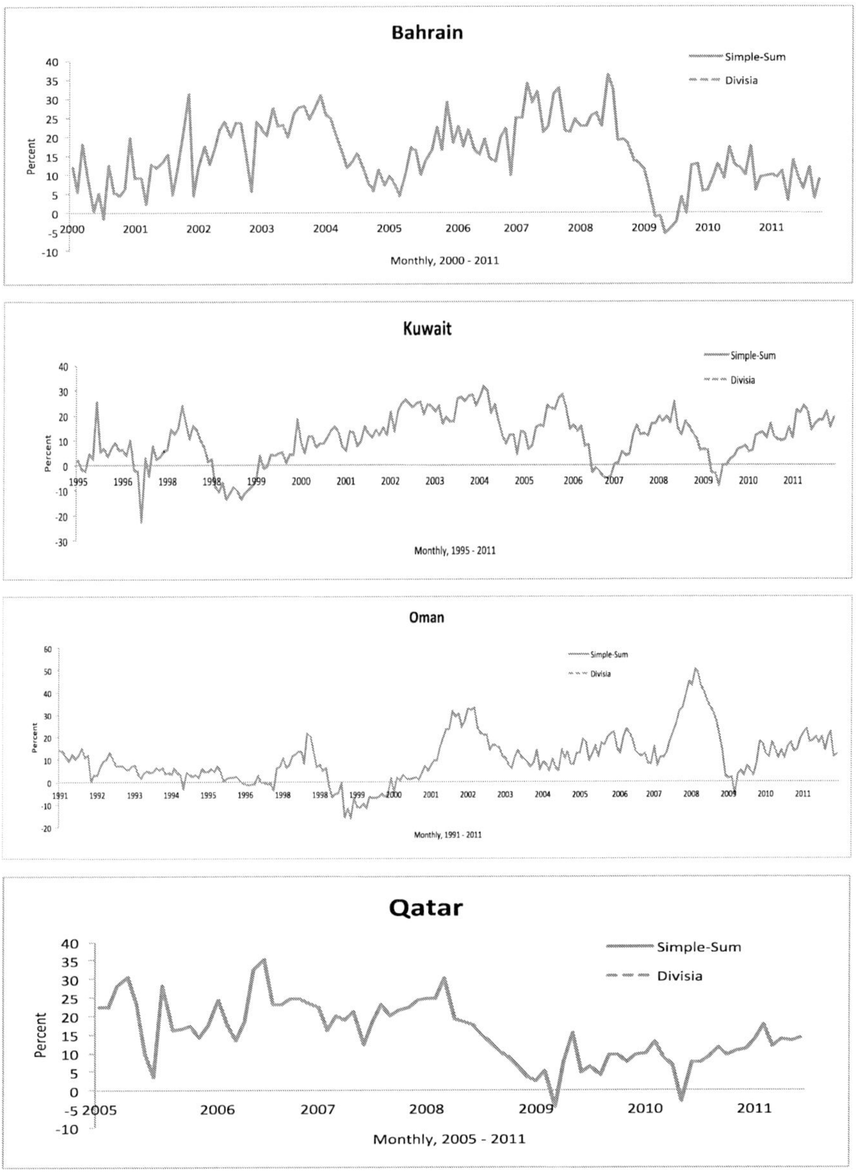

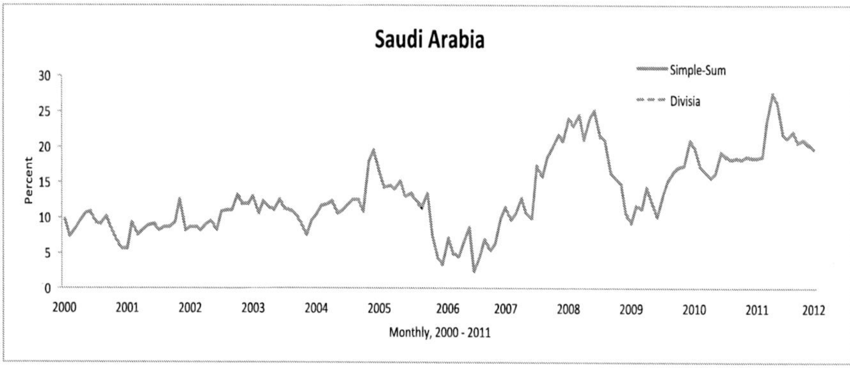
Saudi Arabia
Simple-Sum
Divisia
Percent
30
25
20
15
10
5
0
2000
2001
2002
2003
2004
2005
2006
2007
2008
2009
2010
2011
2012
Monthly, 2000 - 2011

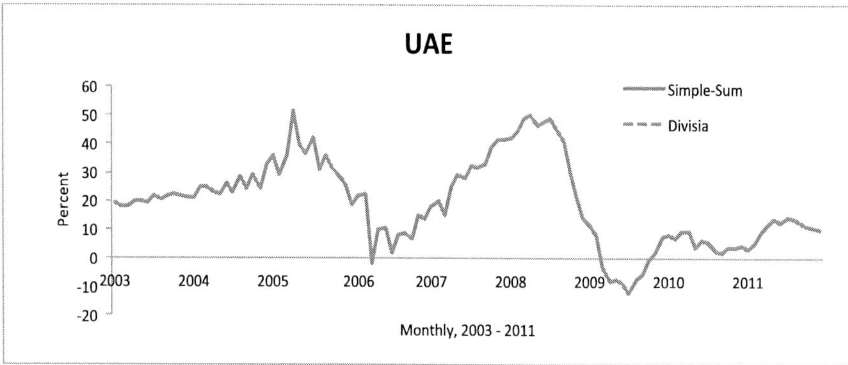
UAE
Simple-Sum
Divisia
Percent
60
50
40
30
20
10
0
-10
-20
2003
2004
2005
2006
2007
2008
2009
2010
2011
Monthly, 2003 - 2011

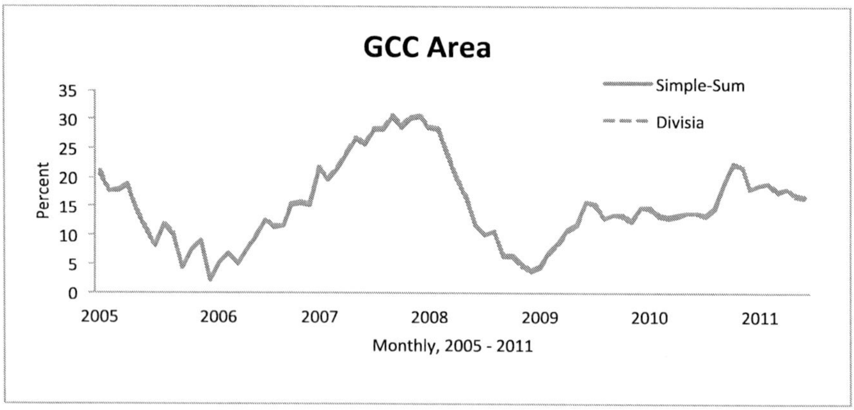
GCC Area
Simple-Sum
Divisia
Percent
35
30
25
20
15
10
5
0
2005
2006
2007
2008
2009
2010
2011
Monthly, 2005 - 2011

Figure 3-2: Year-Over-Year Growth Rates of the Divisia and Simple-Sum Monetary Aggregates, M2 (Annual Percentage Change)

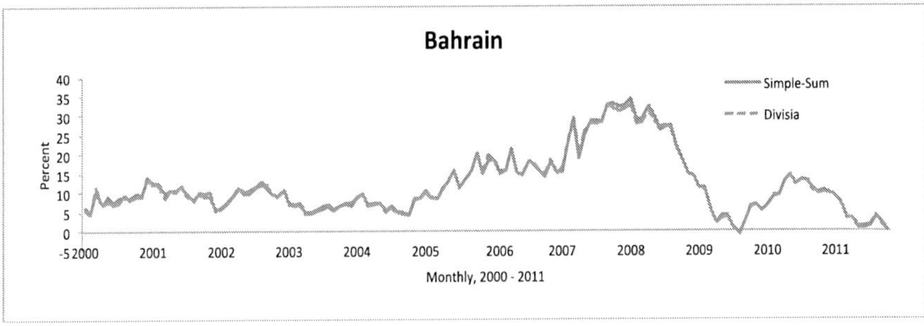

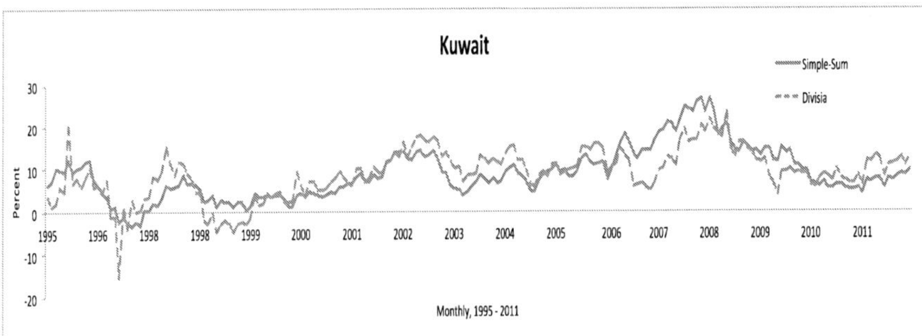

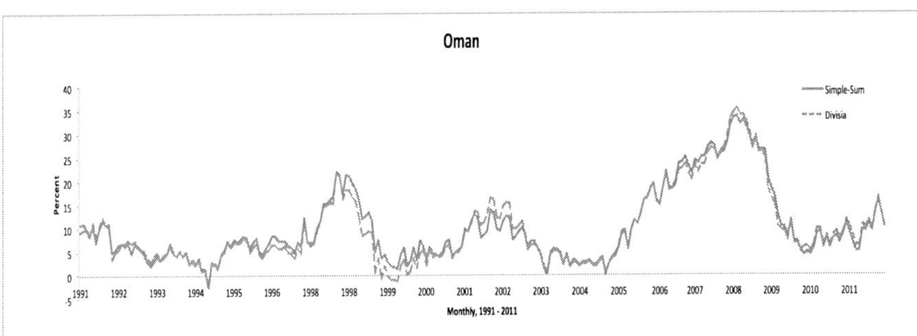

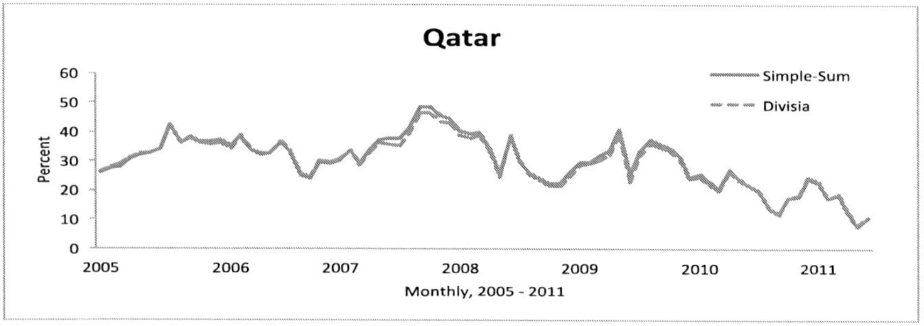
Qatar
60
50
40
30
20
10
0
Percent
Simple-Sum
Divisia
2005
2006
2007
2008
2009
2010
2011
Monthly, 2005 - 2011

Saudi Arabia
30
25
20
15
10
5
0
Percent
Simple-Sum
Divisia
2000
2001
2002
2003
2004
2005
2006
2007
2008
2009
2010
2011
Monthly, 2000 - 2011

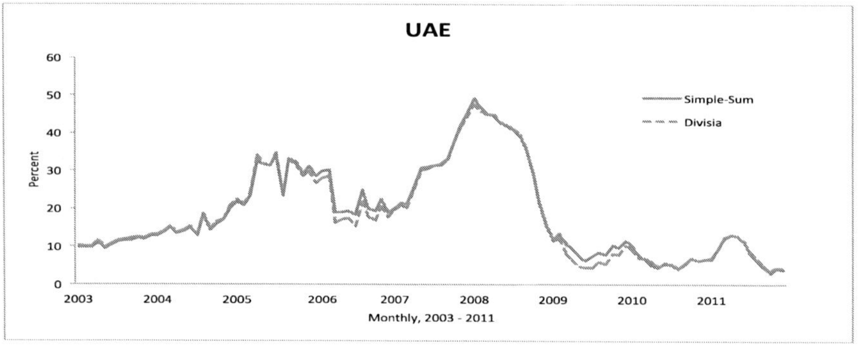
UAE
60
50
40
30
20
10
0
Percent
Simple-Sum
Divisia
2003
2004
2005
2006
2007
2008
2009
2010
2011
Monthly, 2003 - 2011

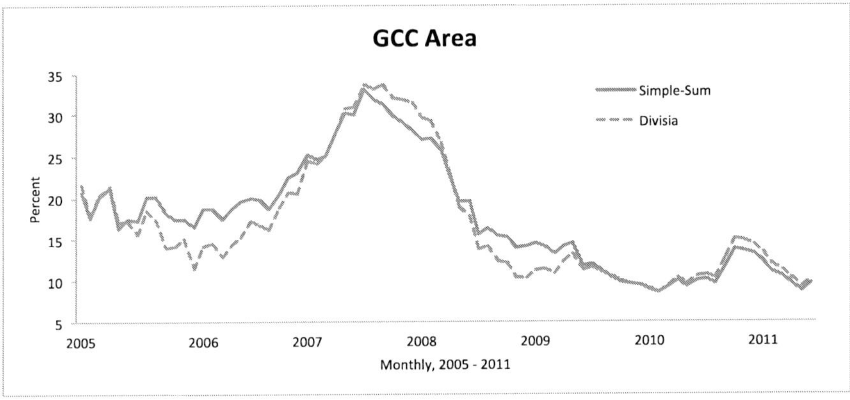
GCC Area
35
30
25
20
15
10
5
Percent
2005
2006
2007
2008
2009
2010
2011
Monthly, 2005 - 2011
Simple-Sum
Divisia

CHAPTER FOUR

A CORE INFLATION INDICATOR FOR THE GULF AREA: A GENERALIZED DYNAMIC FACTOR MODEL APPROACH

4.1 Introduction

The economic policies of the GCC countries are going through critical transitions corresponding to the creation of the central monetary authority for the Gulf area—known as the Gulf Monetary Council (GMC).[1] The GMC will implement a common monetary policy over the GCC countries where a single currency will be circulated in the Gulf area. Indeed, the GMC will be scrutinizing national and area-wide data for monetary policy decisions. The effectiveness of monetary policy is partly conditional on the data used by policymakers at the GMC to make policy decisions. The higher the quality of the data the GMC uses, the higher probability that they will be making well-informed policy decisions. The consumer price indexes (CPI) produced by many monetary authorities, including the GCC central banks, use expenditure-based weighting systems that carry a potential weighing bias. Another problem with the CPI is that it contains some measurement errors, which can lead to measurement bias, as indicated by Bryan and Cecchetti (1994). Collectively, these problems could hinder the objectivity of the CPI.

To measure inflation, the GCC central banks use the year-over-year growth rate of the CPI. Two major drawbacks are associated with the current inflation index. First, it is a lagging indicator since inflation is primarily derived from only past and contemporaneous observations. Hence, using the CPI to construct inflation is less likely to provide insights

[1] The GMC was established in 2010 and it is currently comprised of four countries: Bahrain, Kuwait, Qatar, and Saudi Arabia. The two remaining Gulf countries, namely Oman and UAE, have opted out from the monetary union. See Akhareif and Barnett (2012) for more details about the Gulf Monetary Union.

about the future inflation. Second, inflation indicators are not free from oscillations and other transitory shocks. Thus, inflation indicators can deliver misleading information to the monetary policy. To overcome this problem, economic authorities adopt core inflation indicators for monetary policy.

Constructing the GCC-wide core inflation indicator is of particular importance for economic policy. Economic authorities in general and central banks in specific produce inflation measures because inflation could significantly affect the real economy. A large number of studies have investigated the relationship between inflation and the real economic activities including output and unemployment. In the short run, a contractionary monetary policy shock adversely impacts the real economic activities as indicated by Fischer and Modigliani (1978), Christiano, Eichenbaum, and Evans (1996) and Romer and Romer (1989, 2003). In the long run, it is also possible for the monetary policy shocks to have a permanent effect on the real economic activities. Using a structural vector autoregression (SVAR) model, Bullard and Keating (1995) indicated that permanent inflation shocks positively impact the level of output for low inflation countries.

There are various approaches to construct smooth and less volatile inflation indexes. The trimmed mean (trimming), for instance, is a common approach to measure core inflation. The trimmed means are defined as limited-influence estimators that average only the central portion of a distribution while disregarding the outliers [see Bryan and Cecchetti (1994)]. However, the trimmed mean method is not completely satisfactory. The optimal size of trimming is not determined via recursive estimation within which the trimmed mean is constructed sequentially, but rather through using criterion functions over the full sample—causing estimates to bias toward particular periods [Rich and Steindel (2007)]. As a result, one must exert extra caution when using the trimming index to circumvent any potential estimation bias.

Another measure of core inflation is known as the ex food and energy series. It is achieved by excluding items such as energy and food from an inflation index due to the high volatility associated with their prices. We do not advocate for such an indicator for two reasons. First, the GCC countries are oil producing countries and their economies depend heavily on oil revenues. Indeed higher oil revenues place an upward pressure on the domestic aggregate demand that could deteriorate the purchasing power of the national currencies and eventually raise cost of living [see Wynne (1999)]. Alkhareif and Barnett (2012) have shown that inflation rates in the Gulf area have peaked during periods of booming oil prices.

Second, the Gulf countries, being members of the Organization of the Petroleum Exporting Countries (OPEC), are considered as price makers rather than price takers. In fact, OPEC leaders regularly target future oil prices in their meetings. Based on their price target, they determine proportionally how much each country produces and hence their economies are less likely to be affected by oil shocks. Thus, excluding energy prices would be unreasonable and for these very reasons, we include energy prices in the derivations of our core inflation indicators.

In order to build a GCC-wide price indicator that is free from short-term fluctuations and other noises, we use the Generalized Dynamic Factor Model (GDFM) introduced in Altissimo, Cristadoro, Forni, Lippi, and Veronese (2010). The main premise of the dynamic factor model is that each variable in the dataset can be decomposed into two unobserved orthogonal components: i) the common component which is highly correlated with the remaining macrovariables and ii) the idiosyncratic component which is specific for each variable individually and hence has no effect on other variables [see Cristadoro, Forni, Reichlin, and Veronese (2005)]. The GDFM enables us to remove short-term fluctuations and sector-specific shocks while retaining the long-term components. We construct our core inflation indicators based upon the information embedded in the cross-section and time series characteristics of the variables in the dataset [see Wynne (1999)]. More specifically, our core inflation indicator is constructed by using dual smoothing procedures where first, we perform a cross-sectional smoothing to net out the idiosyncratic (sector specific) component of inflation while maintaining the common component of the national inflation. Second, we apply a time series smoothing by extracting the long-term (longer than one year) common components and hence removing the high frequency movements of the common components [see Altissimo, Cristadoro, Forni, Lippi, and Veronese (2010)].

Building on the work of Alkhareif and Barnett (2012), we provide the Gulf monetary union a core inflation indicator by using Divisia indexes that are directly related to inflation. In particular, we use the Divisia monetary aggregates as well as Divisia price indexes, such as components' user-cost prices, in deriving our core inflation indicators. We name such indicators as "Divisia core inflation indicators". We then compare our Divisia core inflation indicators with the traditional core inflation indicators obtained by using the simple-sum monetary aggregates. To our knowldege, it is the first attempt to the field of aggregation to construct core inflation indicators using the Divisia quantity and price aggregates.

The originality of our core inflation indicator is manifested in the following ways: first, our core inflation indicators use Divisia monetary aggregates that are known for their consistency with aggregation theory and monetary theory. Divisia indexes are also known for their solid microeconomic foundation, in contrast to their simple-sum counterparts. Second, to our knowledge, this is the first core inflation indicator for the overall GCC area. The Gulf Monetary Council (GMC) will benefit from our core inflation indicators in enhancing the Gulf-wide database, whereas economic researchers and financial analysts can use our inflation indexes to carry out various applications and empirical studies. Finally, our core inflation indicator will improve the quality and timeliness of data in the Gulf area, since we use properly constructed monetary aggregates, namely the Divisia indexes. Also, using the GDFM will exploit information on leading variables and hence improve the timeliness of data.

The remainder of this chapter is organized as follows. Section 4.2 provides an overview of the Generalized Dynamic Factor Model and an outline of alternative measures for inflation in the Gulf area. Section 4.3 constructs core inflation indicators for the GCC countries and builds a single core inflation indicator for the GCC area. Section 4.4 compares the performance of the alternative monetary aggregates in forecasting the Gulf inflation. Section 4.5 concludes the chapter.

4.2 Methodology

The motivation of using the Generalized Dynamic Factor Model (GDFM) is that it enables us not only to separate the common shocks from the idiosyncratic counterparts, but also to extract the long-run common component part from the common shocks. It is reasonable to model the Gulf inflation indicators based upon the principle that there are two kinds of shocks a country could face: the common shock and the idiosyncratic (country specific) shock, since most of the oil-producing countries including the GCC states are exposed to global markets. Hence, the GCC countries are more likely to encounter common shocks—although not necessarily at the same time or magnitude. For example, the Gulf countries have experienced a slowdown in economic growth when oil prices plunged in the midst of the financial crisis as a result of a sluggish global demand on oil. This is a clear indication that GCC economies face similar external shocks and hence they have more synchronized business cycles. The boom of the real estate prices in the UAE prior to the financial crisis underscores the existence of sector-specific shocks in the GCC area.

The depreciation of the U.S. dollar, mainly driven by the U.S. Federal Reserves' expansionary monetary policy, is another cause of inflation in the GCC area. During the financial crisis, the GCC countries have witnessed record-high inflation rates for which the GCC-wide inflation rate exceeded 8%.[2] Given the fact that GCC countries except Kuwait maintain a fixed exchange rate against the U.S. dollar, the value of their national currencies will vary correspondingly to movements in the U.S. dollar, implying that the GCC economies are expected to face similar monetary policy shocks.

This section provides an overview of the Generalized Dynamic Factor Model (GDFM) proposed by Altissimo, Cristadoro, Forni, Lippi, and Veronese (2010). It describes the procedure for constructing our core inflation indicators. Altissimo, Cristadoro, Forni, Lippi, and Veronese (2010) outlined a statistical procedure for computing the long-run common component of inflation, consisting of i) estimating the covariance matrices of the common and idiosyncratic components, ii) deriving the static factors (i.e., the generalized principal components of the observed variables), and finally, iii) projecting the long-term common component of inflation on the static factors. Our core inflation indicators are obtained by projecting the long-run common component on a small number of generalized principal components.

Despite the creation of the Gulf monetary council, there is no inflation data available for the overall GCC area. In this paper, we offer two alternative methods for constructing inflation indexes for the Gulf area. The first method is known as the traditional approach, which aggregates the growth rates of national CPIs over countries using GDP weights. This approach of aggregation remains dissatisfactory, due to the inherited ad hoc nature of the GDP weighting method. As indicated by Barnett (2012), the traditional approach of aggregation produces a result that is disconnected from aggregation theory. The other approach aggregates the growth rates of CPIs over countries using Divisia share weights. The Divisia approach of aggregation is consistent with aggregation theory and therefore, we recommend the Gulf monetary council to adopt this method of aggregation to construct aggregate data for the Gulf area.

4.2.1 Generalized Dynamic Factor Model

The Generalized Dynamic Factor Model (GDFM) introduced by Altissimo, Cristadoro, Forni, Lippi, and Veronese (2010) is applied on our large-dimensional dataset within which economic variables display strong

---

[2] See Alkhareif and Barnett (2012) for more information about inflation rates in the GCC area.

comovements among themselves. Recent empirical studies suggest that GDFM perform well in large cross-sectional datasets, especially when the number of cross-sectional series is larger than the number of time series observations [see, e.g., Stock and Watson (2011) and Cristadoro, Forni, Reichlin, and Veronese (2005)]. The GDFM framework enables us to identify sources of price fluctuations by using a few common factors, which can explain a large proportion of the covariation across economic series. The main advantage of using GDFM is that it separates long-term movements of variables from short-term fluctuations. Let $\mathbf{x}_t = \mathbf{x}_t = (x_{1t}, \dots, x_{nt})', t \in \mathbb{Z},$ be a zero-mean stationary process vector with finite second-order moments. The underlying premise of the dynamic factor models is that each variable, $x_{it}, i \in \mathbb{N},$ can be decomposed into the sum of two stationary, mutually orthogonal, unobservable components, known as the common component χ_{it}, and the idiosyncratic component ξ_{it}:

$$x_{it} = \chi_{it} + \xi_{it} \tag{4.1}$$

The idiosyncratic component represents a variable specific shock which does not impact other variables in the system. In contrast, the common component underlines the principle embedded in GDFM that variables are more likely to be driven by few common shocks which influence the comovements of variables. Unlike the traditional factor models where each idiosyncratic component is orthogonal to the others in the cross-section, the GDFM permits a limited amount of correlation between idiosyncratic components. Forni, Hallin, Lippi, and Reichlin (2000) imposed the total amount of cross-correlation assumption to ensure that this amount is large for the common components, as opposed to the idiosyncratic counterparts. In particular, they assumed that the first q eigenvalues of the spectral density matrices of the common components diverge in the frequency interval $[-\pi, \pi]$, as opposed to the remaining eigenvalues. This will guarantee a minimum amount of cross-correlation between the common components. By assuming that the first idiosyncratic eigenvalue of the spectral density matrix of the idiosyncratic components is uniformly bounded, a limited amount of cross-correlation between the idiosyncratic components is also guaranteed.[3] Mathematically, the common component is defined as the linear combination of the common shocks:

[3] See Forni, Hallin, Lippi, and Reichlin (2000) for a more rigorous formulation about the GDFM assumptions.

$$\chi_{it} = b_{i1}(L)u_{1t} + b_{i2}(L)u_{2t} + \cdots + b_{iq}(L)u_{qt} \tag{4.2}$$

where u_{jt} $(j = 1, \ldots, q)$ is the jth common shock, and $b(L)_{jt}$ is the corresponding coefficient within which L denotes the lag operator.

A clear advantage of this common component formulation (4.2) is that while unobservable common shocks are the same for all variables, their coefficients are different, allowing variables to react differently to those shocks. It is useful to our purpose in constructing core inflation to have this flexibility because we can then determine the dynamics between variables and inflation. In particular, variables in the system can be leading, coincident, or lagged (i.e. shocks are loaded with delay) with respect to inflation [see Cristadoro, Forni, Reichlin, and Veronese (2005)]. By analyzing the dynamics between inflation and a large number of variables in the dataset, we can make inferences about future (unobservable) inflation by using the information embedded in variables leading inflation. Therefore, it is possible to predict inflation by exploiting information from the current values of the leading variables. Consider the following static representation form of the common components:

$$\chi_{it} = c_{i1}F_{1t} + c_{i2}F_{2t} + \cdots + c_{ir}F_{rt} \tag{4.3}$$

where $F_{jt}(j = 1, \ldots, r)$ is the jth static factor and c_{jt} is its corresponding factor loading.

The static factors in (4.3) are generally unknown and hence, have to be estimated. To overcome this problem, Altissimo, Cristadoro, Forni, Lippi, and Veronese (2010) proposed a method of estimating the factors as linear combinations of the observable variables. It involved forming a set of r variables to form a basis for the linear space spanned by the factors. Based on this method, we estimate the factors as the generalized principal components of the observed variables using the contemporaneous variance-covariance matrices of the long-term and short-term common components as well as the idiosyncratic components. The generalized principal components are the contemporaneous linear combinations of the observable variables with the smallest variance ratio of the short-term common component plus the idiosyncratic component and the long-term common component, suggesting that they can consistently approximate the long-term common components as $n, T \to \infty$. Because we only use contemporaneous values of the variables in the dataset, there will not be an end-of-sample deterioration usually associated with band pass filters used to extract the long-term components [see Altissimo, Cristadoro, Forni,

Lippi, and Veronese (2010) for a proof]. The subsequent section provides a thorough discussion regarding the estimation procedure of the long-term common components.

It is worth mentioning that the number of common shocks (dynamic factors) q and the number of static factors r in equations (4.2) and (4.3), respectively, are generally unknown and thereby must be estimated.[4] To estimate the number of dynamic factors, we use the techniques provided by Hallin and Liska (2007) and we employ the criterion by Bai and Ng (2002) to determine the number of the static factors.[5] To our knowledge, Hallin-Liska's criterion is the only measure that can determine the number of dynamic factors without imposing the finite number of static factors assumption—therefore Hallin-Liska's criterion is considered the most accurate measure.[6] We apply the information criterion to two separate datasets, as we independently construct the Divisia core inflation indicator and the traditional core inflation indicator. The estimation results in our analysis indicate that the number of dynamic factors q and the number of static factors r for both indicators are $q = 3$ and $r = 45$.[7]

A key issue confronting monetary authorities and economic agencies is how to construct a reliable inflation indicator, which provides a valid assessment of the outlook for price developments. It is crucial to have an inflation indicator that is free from errors and transitory turbulences. The existence of, for instance, measurement errors and short-term oscillations could hinder the objectivity of the inflation indicator, misleading policymakers to make misguided policy decisions. The less responsive the core inflation indicator is to transitory shocks and seasonal noise, the better off the central banks are in monitoring inflation. We construct core

4 The numbers of dynamic factors q and static factors r are linked together via the number of lags, s, for which $r = q(s + 1)$. Under our static representation assumption, the common component which is driven by q dynamic factors can also be expressed as a linear combination of r static factors. See Forni, Hallin, Lippi, and Reichlin (2000) for a more complete discussion.

5 We would like to thank Roman Liska for providing us with the Matlab codes needed to estimate the number of dynamic factors.

6 See Forni and Lippi (2011) for an analytical comparison between various estimation procedures.

7 In order to apply Hallin–Liska and Bai–Ng panel criteria (PC_p), one must stipulate an upper bound on the number of the dynamic factors q_{max} and the static factors r_{max}, respectively. We have altered our choice of q_{max} and r_{max} several times to ensure consistent estimates of the number of the factors. See Hallin and Liska (2007) and Bai and Ng (2002) for more details about the alternative methods of estimation.

inflation indicators that are free from short-term fluctuations by using statistical techniques involving spectral decomposition [see, e.g., Stock and Watson (2003)]. Like any stationary variable, the common component can be decomposed into short-term component, χ_{it}^{S}, and long-term component, χ_{it}^{L}:

$$\chi_{it} = \chi_{it}^{L} + \chi_{it}^{S} \tag{4.4}$$

Of course, the long-term common component, χ_{it}^{L}, remains theoretical and hence unobservable. Our goal is to estimate the long-term common component for inflation. We describe the estimation procedure in the following section.

4.2.2 Estimating the Long-Term Common Components

The Generalized Dynamic Factor Model (GDFM) introduced by Altissimo, Cristadoro, Forni, Lippi, and Veronese (2010) involves the generalized principal components analysis, as well as the frequency domain methods. The framework of our GDFM enables us to transform the dataset from time domain into frequency domain via Fourier transformation technique, where functions of time can be converted into a sum of a (possibly infinite) number of waves. The time domain and the frequency domain provide two alternative representations to the same dynamic system and hence we can use them interchangeably without giving up valuable information. To transform the frequency domain back to the time domain, we simply apply the inverse Fourier transform. The merit of using spectrum analysis is that it enables us to discover "hidden" information of a large panel of data. Specifically, we can exploit superior information embedded in the cross-sectional dimension using a few common factors that can explain a large proportion of the covariation across macroeconomic series [see Altissimo, Cristadoro, Forni, Lippi, and Veronese (2010)].

Let $\mathbf{x}_t = (x_{1t}, \dots, x_{nt})', t \in \mathbb{Z}$, be a vector of observable variables in the dataset and let $\hat{\Sigma}_x(k)$ be the cross-covariance matrix of the observable variables estimated with lags $k = -M, \dots, M$. We estimate the spectral density matrix of the observable variables, $\hat{S}_x(\theta_j)$, by applying a discrete-time Fourier transformation to the covariance matrix of the observable variables $\hat{\Sigma}_x(k)$. Let J be the number of points where the spectrum $\hat{S}_x(\theta_j)$ is estimated. We multiply the covariance matrices $\hat{\Sigma}_x(k)$ by the Bartlett lag-window estimator as follows:

$$\hat{S}_x(\theta_j) = \frac{1}{2\pi}\Sigma_{k=-M}^{M} W_k \hat{\Sigma}_x(k) e^{-i\theta_j k}$$

where $W_k = 1 - \frac{|k|}{M+1}$ and $\theta_j = \frac{2\pi j}{2J+1}, j = -J, \dots, J$. In order to invert the spectrum on a band, the number of points, J, ought to be large enough to have points within the relevant band. To ensure that the spectral density matrix of $\mathbf{x}_t$ is positive semi-definite, our choice of M is based on the fixed rule $M = M(T) = round(\sqrt{T})$.[8] Hence, we set $M = 7$ and $J = 63$.

Using the dynamic principal component decomposition, the spectral density matrix of the observable variables can be decomposed into the spectral density matrices of the common component and the idiosyncratic component:

$$S_x(\theta) = S_\chi(\theta) + S_\xi(\theta)$$

Furthermore, the spectral density matrix of the common component can be decomposed into the spectral density matrices of the long-term common component and the short-term common component:

$$S_\chi(\theta) = S_{\chi^L}(\theta) + S_{\chi^S}(\theta)$$

The eigenvalues of the spectral density matrix $\hat{S}_x(\theta_j)$ convey useful information of variance in the system. The largest eigenvalue has the largest variance, thereby it contains more information about the comovement between variables. It is possible then to utilize the information from an extremely large dataset and explore the dynamics between the variables and inflation by using fewer entries. More specifically, we can apply proper procedure to reduce the dimensionality of the problem while maintaining an accurate inference about inflation. We follow the procedure proposed by Altissimo, Cristadoro, Forni, Lippi, and Veronese (2010) to obtain the spectral density matrix of the common components. The procedure consists of the following four steps:

Step 1: compute the eigenvalues $\lambda_j(\theta), (j = 1, \dots, n)$ and eigenvectors, $U_j(\theta)$, of the spectral density matrix $\hat{S}_x(\theta_j)$

---

[8] See Hallin and Liska (2007) and Forni, Hallin, Lippi, and Reichlin (2000) for more details about the method of selecting the size of Bartlett lag window.

Step 2: sort the eigenvalues from the highest to lowest and correspondingly rearrange the eigenvectors

Step 3: estimate the number of common factors q by applying the statistical technique developed by Hallin and Liska (2007)[9]

Step 4: construct the $(q \times q)$ diagonal matrix, $\Lambda(\theta)$ having the first q largest eigenvalues $\lambda_1(\theta), \ldots, \lambda_q(\theta)$ on the diagonal and build the $(n \times q)$ matrix, $U(\theta)$, of the corresponding eigenvectors

$$U(\theta) = [U_1(\theta) U_2(\theta) \cdots U_q(\theta)]$$

The spectral density matrix of the common components is defined as:

$$\hat{S}_\chi(\theta) = U(\theta)\Lambda(\theta)\tilde{U}(\theta) \tag{4.5}$$

where the tilde indicates the conjugation.

It is possible to recover the covariance matrix of common components by applying the inverse discrete Fourier transform to equation (4.5). This returns the estimated covariance matrix of common components:

$$\hat{\Sigma}_\chi = \frac{2\pi}{2J+1} \Sigma_{j=-J}^{J} \hat{S}_\chi(\theta_j)$$

We can also obtain the covariance matrices of the long-term common components, $\hat{\Sigma}_{\chi L}$, and the short-term common components, $\hat{\Sigma}_{\chi S}$, by applying the inverse discrete Fourier transform to the spectral density matrix of common components $\hat{S}_\chi(\theta)$ over the frequency intervals $\left[0, \frac{\pi}{6}\right]$ and $\left[\frac{\pi}{6}, \pi\right]$, respectively.

Given that we acquired both $\hat{\Sigma}_x$ and $\hat{\Sigma}_\chi$, estimating the variance-covariance matrix of idiosyncratic components is achieved by:

$$\hat{\Sigma}_\xi = diag(\hat{\Sigma}_x - \hat{\Sigma}_\chi)$$

where $diag$ refers to the diagonal matrix within which the off-diagonal entries are zero.

In order to derive the generalized principal components, we compute the generalized eigenvectors $\mathbf{v}_k$ and the corresponding generalized

---

9 See Cristadoro, Forni, Reichlin, and Veronese (2005) for alternative methods.

eigenvalues λ_k of the pair of matrices $(\hat{\Sigma}_{\chi^L}, \hat{\Sigma}_{\chi^S} + \hat{\Sigma}_{\xi})$ solving the generalized eigenvalue problem:[10]

$$\hat{\Sigma}_{\chi^L}\mathbf{v}_k = \lambda_k(\hat{\Sigma}_{\chi^S} + \hat{\Sigma}_{\xi})\mathbf{v}_k \tag{4.6}$$

with the normalization constraints $\mathbf{v}_k'(\hat{\Sigma}_{\chi^S} + \hat{\Sigma}_{\xi})\mathbf{v}_k = 1$. We rearrange the eigenvalues in a decreasing sequence along with their eigenvectors, then we apply the panel criterion proposed in Bai and Ng (2002) to estimate the dimension of the factor space r. Using the generalized eigenvectors in (4.6), the generalized principal components can be defined as:

$$w_{kt} = \mathbf{v}_k'\mathbf{x}_t \tag{4.7}$$

for $k = 1, \cdots, r$.

It is worthwhile to mention that the factors in (4.7) contain information regarding variables that are leading inflation. Thus, we can use such factors as proxies for unavailable future observations and hence avoiding end-of-sample bias typically caused by standard band pass filters [see Altissimo, Cristadoro, Forni, Lippi, and Veronese (2010)]. Estimating the long-term common component, χ_{it}^L, is now straightforward. We project the long-term common component onto suitable linear combinations of the observable variables through which we can maintain long-term waves and remove the short-term ones. More formally, let $\mathbf{V} = (\mathbf{v}_1 \cdots \mathbf{v}_r)$ be a $(n \times r)$ matrix of the generalized eigenvectors and let $\mathbf{w}_t = (w_{1t} \cdots w_{rt})' = \mathbf{V}'\mathbf{x}_t$ be the column vector of the first r generalized principal components where r is the number of static factors obtained by using Bai and Ng's criterion. Finally, the long-term common component is estimated by:

$$\widehat{\chi_t^L} = \hat{\Sigma}_{\chi^L}\mathbf{V}\left(\mathbf{V}'\hat{\Sigma}_x\mathbf{V}\right)^{-1}\boldsymbol{w}_t \tag{4.8}$$

4.2.3 Constructing Inflation Indexes for the Gulf Area

In the aftermath of the 2007-08 financial crisis, when the short-term nominal interest rate reached zero, a number of central banks adopted unconventional monetary policy tools such as quantitative easing, where

---

[10] See Cristadoro, Saporito, and Venditti (2012) for more details and see Cristadoro, Forni, Reichlin, and Veronese (2005) for an alternative representation of the generalized eigenvalue problem.

central banks injected money via purchases of long-term government bonds to stimulate their economies. Using the officially published simple-sum monetary aggregates to measure monetary service flows of the economy can be misleading, since the simple-sum indexes implicitly assume that all components are perfect one-for-one substitutes in producing liquidity services. For example, broad monetary aggregates, which group currency with those that bear positve returns, such as savings and time deposits, will certainly fail to satisfy the perfect substitutiblity assumption. A major advantage of using the Divisia indexes is that the Divisia indexes remove the investment motive and measure all other monetary services associated with economic liquidity, by allowing the weights of monetary assets to vary depending on their monetary services at the margin [Alkhareif and Barnett (2012)]. Therefore, Divisia monetary aggregates provide a reliable measure for liquidity in the economy.

Based upon aggregation theory and statistical index number theory, Alkhareif and Barnett (2012) constructed Divisia monetary aggregates for the GCC area and proposed Divisia-based economic stability indicators. Divisia index, being exact for the quadratic translog specification of the true aggregator function, is indeed a superlative index number.[11] The simple-sum index is neither a superlative index number nor consistent with microeconomic theory and aggregation theory. A large number of studies have confirmed the usefulness of Divisia indexes in forecasting inflation [see, e.g., Binner, Bissoondeeal, Elger, Jones, and Mullineux (2009)].

To date, the Gulf monetary Council (GMC) has not published inflation data for the GCC area. We propose two approaches for measuring inflation in the GCC area: (i) the traditional approach and (ii) the Divisia aggregation approach, in order to illustrate the superiority of the Divisia approach. The former approach aggregates the growth rates of consumer price indexes over countries by using GDP weights. Let K be the number of countries in the Gulf monetary union. For each country $k \in \{1, \ldots, K\}$, define the true cost-of-living index as $p_k^* = p_k^*(\boldsymbol{p_k})$, where $\boldsymbol{p_k} = \boldsymbol{p_k}(t)$ represents the vector of prices of consumer goods at time t. Let e_k be country $k's$ currency exchange rate against a market basket of currencies. The Gulf area's traditional inflation, π_t, is defined as:

$$\pi_t = \Sigma_{k=1}^{K} h_{kt} \left[log(p_{kt}^* e_{kt}) - log(p_{k,t-1}^* e_{k,t-1}) \right] \quad (4.9)$$

[11] See Diewet (1976), Barnett (1982), and Barnett (2012) for a more complete discussion about the properties of superlative index numbers.

where h_k is country $k's$ GDP share in the Gulf Monetary Union. The GDP weights are known for being ad hoc weights that are inconsistent with aggregation theory. As indicated by Barnett (2007), using ad hoc weights to aggregate over countries does not produce nesting of the multilateral or unilateral representative agent approaches. To overcome this problem, Barnett (2007) suggested deriving weights using aggregation theory and index number theory. For each country $k \in \{1, \ldots, K\}$, let M_k^* be the real per-capita monetary services aggregate, M_k be the nominal per-capita monetary services aggregate, Π_k^* be the real user-cost price aggregate, and Π_k be the nominal user-cost price aggregate.[12] Let s_k be country $k's$ share of total GCC area population. The expenditure shares, d_k, of country k of the Gulf union's monetary service flow is obtained by using Divisia monetary aggregates and Divisia aggregate user-cost prices for each country. More formally, the kth country's expenditure shares of the Gulf union's monetary service flow are defined as:[13]

$$d_k = \frac{M_k^* \Pi_k^* p_k^* e_k s_k}{\sum_{k=1}^{K} M_k^* \Pi_k^* p_k^* e_k s_k} = \frac{M_k \Pi_k^* e_k s_k}{\sum_{k=1}^{K} M_k \Pi_k^* e_k s_k} = \frac{M_k^* \Pi_k e_k s_k}{\sum_{k=1}^{K} M_k^* \Pi_k e_k s_k}$$

where $0 \le d_k \le 1$ and $\Sigma_{k=1}^{K} d_k = 1$.

The Gulf area's Divisia inflation index, π_t^D, is defined as:

$$\pi_t^D = \Sigma_{k=1}^{K} d_{kt} \left[log(p_{kt}^* e_{kt}) - log(p_{k,t-1}^* e_{k,t-1}) \right] \quad (4.10)$$

Figure 4-1 depicts the inflation rates for the Gulf area using the two alternative approaches of weighting inflation across countries.[14] To take a closer look at the price developments between the U.S. and the Gulf area, we include the annual inflation rate for the United States. As we expected, inflation rates for the U.S. and the Gulf area exhibit similar trends, given the fact that GCC countries, except Kuwait, maintain a fixed exchange rate against the U.S. dollar. Although inflation rates for the U.S. and the Gulf area exhibit strong comovements, inflation rates in the GCC area stand above their counterparts most of the time. In fact, the gap between the U.S. and the GCC area's inflation rates widen the most during the recent

[12] A complete display of the Divisia quantity and price indexes along with alternative share weights formulations is provided in Barnett (2007).

[13] See Barnett (2007) for alternative methods of weighting inflation across countries.

[14] See Alkhareif and Barnett (2012) for a recent application to construct Divisia inflation index for the Gulf area.

financial crisis. In 2009, the U.S. had a deflationary episode and there was a corresponding decline in inflation rates for the Gulf countries. Inflation rates in the Gulf area exemplify the movements in oil prices that peaked in mid-2008 and plunged subsequently as a result of distress over the global economy. This clearly signifies the important role oil prices play on influencing the price developments in the GCC area.

4.3 A Core Inflation indicator for the GCC Area

The formation of the Gulf Monetary Council (GMC) necessitates constructing area-wide statistics essential for the Gulf common currency area. Policymakers at the GMC expect to use a large number of national data and GCC-wide indexes to monitor the economic stance in the Gulf area and to make well-informed monetary policy decisions. Strengthening national statistical agencies is essential to increase the quality and timeliness of national data, thereby improving monetary policy in the region. The GMC is anticipated to create a unified statistical system (equivalent to Eurostat) to provide the monetary union with high quality GCC-wide data.[15] The main goals of this paper are to provide core inflation indicators for the GCC countries as well as to build a single core inflation indicator for the Gulf area. In this regard, our core inflation indicators will provide the Gulf central banks with additional statistics that are useful for monetary policy. Our data will also help financial analysts and economic agents explore price developments in the Gulf area and more importantly the interaction between Gulf inflation and other macroeconomic variables.

It is possible to identify the sources of price fluctuations since the Generalized Dynamic Factor Model (GDFM) enables us to distinguish between common shocks and idiosyncratic shocks. By identifying the sources of shocks, the policymakers have more information on how to respond to different shocks. For the Gulf monetary union, it is the common shocks that matter for the monetary policy, because these shocks symmetrically affect countries, although possibly with different magnitudes. The idiosyncratic shocks not only contain measurement errors that can lead to measurement bias, but also exhibit a weak correlation with financial variables and real economic indicators, especially the long-term movements of inflation [see, e.g., Cristadoro, Forni, Reichlin, and Veronese (2005)]. Eliminating the idiosyncratic shocks from our core

[15] For more information about the objectives of the Gulf monetary union, visit the Gulf monetary council website at http://www.en.gmco.int.

inflation indicators shall lead to a more reliable core inflation measure. In this regard, our core inflation indicators provide useful tools for policymakers that they could use to strengthen monetary policy at the Gulf monetary union.

We advocate including oil prices to construct the GCC core inflation indicators since oil revenues are the driving-engine for most economies in the GCC area. In fact, a large portion of government spending in the GCC area is finance via oil revenues rather than using standard fiscal policy tools such as imposing taxes and issuing government debt. The massive government spending on infrastructure projects and social programs could increase domestic prices. In early to mid-2008 oil prices surged, implying higher revenues for most GCC countries from oil exports. Nevertheless, the surging oil prices triggered a record high inflation rate for which the overall GCC area inflation reached 8% in mid 2008 as indicated by Alkhareif and Barnett (2012). Since inflation rates in the GCC area are primarily driven by oil prices, it is inappropriate to disregard energy prices from core inflation. By taking into consideration the variations in oil prices, our core inflation indicators provide a more accurate outlook on the future price developments in the Gulf area, therefore helping policymakers make well-informed decisions.

In this section, we construct core inflation indicators for the GCC countries and recursively build a core inflation indicator for the Gulf area. We use the Generalized Dynamic Factor Model (GDFM) intrduced by Forni, Hallin, Lippi, and Reichlin (2000) and further developed by Altissimo, Cristadoro, Forni, Lippi, and Veronese (2010). Monetary aggregates play a pivotal role in constructing our core inflation indicators. The core inflation indicator for the GCC area is computed using two separate monetary aggregates: i) the traditional simple-sum monetary aggregates, and ii) the Divisia monetary aggregates. Our hypothesis here is that Divisia indexes, which are based upon microeconomic theory and consistent with aggregation and index number theory, can provide more accurate core inflation indicators for the Gulf area. Generally speaking, an abundance of liquidity in the GCC economies tends to cause an upward pressure on inflation. The Divisia aggregation approach weights the components according to their usefulness in transaction, thus Divisia monetary indexes provide a reliable measure of the liquidity in the economy. Divisia indexes, such as Divisia user-cost aggregates as well as the components' user costs, can signal economic disruptions such as the recent financial crisis, as indicated in Alkhareif and Barnett (2012). In addition, these variables offer valuable information pertaining to financial markets' harmonization as well as measuring the effectiveness of monetary policy over countries [see, e.g., Barnett (2007)]. Hence, we advocate using Divisia indexes to measure the core inflation in the GCC area.

4.3.1 Data Descriptions and Sources

We use a 461 cross-sectional series to construct the Divisia core inflation indicator and a 353 cross-sectional series to construct the traditional core inflation indicator, with monthly data from June 2004 to December 2011. The data were extracted from various sources such as the GCC central banks, International Financial Statistics (IFS), Federal Reserve Economic Data (FRED), Bloomberg database, and the GCC Secretariat General. To construct our core inflation indicators, we use prices including consumer price indexes (CPI) and producer prices. Variables such as exchange rates and oil prices are also included in the computations of our core inflation indicators. We also use the interest rates on different types of financial assets including overnight deposits, demand deposits, savings and time deposits, and quasi-money. Government bonds and interest rate spreads are also included in the dataset. The output data for the GCC countries are only available in annual series. To obtain monthly output series, we use the state-space model for interpolation introduced by Stock and Watson (2010). In particular, we use monthly oil exports and non-oil exports to interpolate the annual observations of oil GDP and non-oil GDP, respectively.

Prior to the analysis, we normalized the original data by subtracting their means and dividing by their standard deviations. There were not many missing data in our study. We applied moving average interpolation, whenever data were missing. A key condition for using any dynamic factor model, especially for estimating the spectral matrix of the data, is the statinarity of variables in the system [see Forni and Lippi (2011) for more details]. To ensure statinarity of the variables in our datasets, we transform the non-stationary variables into a stationary series using proper transformation. For instance, we log difference the variables in the dataset with I(1) cointegration. Non-stationary variables that have negative values were only differenced. We then apply Augmented Dickey Fuller (ADF) and Phillips Perron (PP) unit root tests to confirm their stationarity.[16] All quantities have been seasonally adjusted using the X11 procedure.

---

[16] Since we have a total of 485 variables in our study, including the results of the standard unit root tests is not feasible. The overall results of the unit root tests are provided upon request.

Lastly, when constructing the Divisia core inflation indicators, we use Divisia monetary aggregates for the GCC countries instead of the simple-sum monetary aggregates. We also use other Divisia indexes such as monetary assets' user-cost prices, Divisia user-cost aggregates, and dual prices. We obtained the Divisia monetary aggregates as well as the economic stability indicators from Alkhareif and Barnett (2012).

4.3.2 Constructing Core Inflation Indicators for the GCC Countries

It is worthwhile to mention that, currently, maintaining price stability is not the ultimate monetary policy target of the GCC central banks. With the exception of Kuwait, all the GCC central banks maintain a fixed exchange rate against the U.S. dollar and allow free capital flows in and out of their countries. Therefore, these countries have forgone independence of their monetary policy. Even though inflation is not the target variable by GCC central banks, providing core inflation indicators is essential for strengthening economic policy in the Gulf area—especially since inflation can permanently impact real economic activities [see Bullard and Keating (1995)].

Giving up monetary policy independence does not mean that the central banks cannot control inflation. Lim, Columba, Costa, Kongsamut, Otani, Saiyid, Wezel, and Wu (2011) investigated the effectiveness of the macroprudential instruments in monetary policy by using the panel regression analysis including the Generalized Method of Moments (GMM). Their findings suggest that macroprudential instruments are indeed effective in simultaneously reducing systemic risk and strengthening the banking system. Hence, the GCC central banks can use different macroprudential policy tools involving capital requirements, loan provisioning, and can constrict financial regulations alone with banking supervision—all of which can affect inflation.

Fiscal policy also plays a major role in influencing inflation. As we mentioned earlier, government expenditure financed by oil revenues puts an upward pressure on domestic prices, and hence tightening the fiscal policy reduces inflation. Since the purpose of this paper is to supply the GCC central banks with core inflation indicators, rather than evaluating alternative policy rules, we provide our results of alternative inflation indicators, regardless of policy limitations.

Let K be the number of countries in the Gulf area. For each country $k \in \{1, \dots, K\}$, let $\tilde{p}_{kt}$ and $\tilde{p}_{kt}^{D}$ be the long-term common component of CPI obtained using the traditional (simple-sum) and Divisia monetary aggregates, respectively. Define the kth country's traditional core inflation indicator $\tilde{\pi}_{kt}$ and Divisia core inflation indicator $\tilde{\pi}^{D}_{kt}$, respectively, by:[17]

$$\tilde{\pi}_{kt} = log\ \tilde{p}_{kt} - log\ \tilde{p}_{k,t-1}$$

and

$$\tilde{\pi}^{D}_{kt} = log\ \tilde{p}^{D}_{kt} - log\ \tilde{p}^{D}_{k,t-1}$$

The traditional core inflation indicator uses the simple-sum monetary aggregates which are obtained by simply summing up all monetary assets within an aggregate with unity share weights. The main premise of the simple-sum monetary aggregation approach is that monetary assets within an aggregate are one-to-one perfect substitutes. The perfect substitutability assumption is found to be unrealistic particularly for broader aggregates where liquid assets like currency are grouped with less liquid assets such as savings and time deposits. However, the Divisia core inflation indicator uses the Divisia monetary aggregates along with the Divisia price aggregates. The Divisia monetary aggregates weights the components according to their usefulness in transaction and hence monetary assets within an aggregate are not necessarily perfect substitutes. Thus, the Divisia core inflation indicators are a more reliable measure of price developments in the GCC area.

To measure inflation, the GCC central banks use the year-over-year growth rate of the CPI.[18] For each country, we compare our core inflation indicators with the inflation measures supplied by the GCC central banks. Figure 4-2 displays the inflation rates and the alternative core inflation indicators for the GCC countries estimated using monthly data over the period June 2004 to December 2011. For each country, our core inflation indicators are more stable than countries' official inflation measures, since the former were constructed by applying a twofold smoothing procedures, namely the cross-sectional and intertemporal smoothing procedures. Being free from short-term fluctuations and transitory shocks, our indicators serve well policymakers in the GCC central banks, especially in monitoring price developments in the GCC countries.

---

[17] To compute the core inflation indicators, we denormalize the transformed data by multiplying the long–term common component of inflation by the standard deviation of the original inflation and adding the mean of the original inflation.

[18] Despite the fact that the year–over–year inflation rate measure is used by central banks worldwide as a measure of inflation, it remains dissatisfactory due to the inherited backward looking nature of such a measure. See Wynne (1999) for a more complete discussion.

For each country, we analyze the behavioral pattern of the alternative core inflation indicators with respect to the officially published inflation. In Bahrain, the Divisia core inflation indicator has been more stable than the traditional core inflation in most of the periods. The traditional core inflation has rotated from being above the Divisia core inflation from early 2010 to the beginning of 2011 and below the Divisia core inflation afterwards—suggesting that the Divisia core inflation indicator provides a more stable measure of inflation (Figure 4-2). In the past couple of years, inflation fluctuated between around -2% and 3% and the traditional core inflation exhibited similar movements, whereas Divisia core inflation has been stable at around 1%.

In Kuwait, the Divisia core inflation remains more stable than its counterpart the traditional core inflation throughout the entire period (Figure 4-2). Unlike the traditional core inflation, the Divisia core inflation has been less responsive to price shocks manifested in the decline of inflation rates in 2006-07 and 2010, as well as the inflation rate hikes during 2008-2009.

Similar results are obtained for Oman for which the Divisia core inflation has been more stable than the traditional core inflation—especially during the financial crisis when inflation reached high record rates exceeding 13% (Figure 4-2). Moreover, the Divisia core inflation did not respond to the price shock in 2010, as opposed to the traditional core measure.

In Qatar, inflation exhibits two distinct phases centered around the financial crisis (Figure 4-2). Starting from 2005, the inflation in Qatar has been in an upward trajectory until the midst of the financial crisis where inflation rates began to decline. Prior to the financial crisis, the traditional core inflation has fluctuated around from being above the Divisia core inflation in mid-2005 to 2006 and below the Divisia core inflation from 2007 to 2008. Afterwards, the traditional core inflation has also altered from being below the Divisia core inflation in 2009 to 2010 and above the Divisia core inflation in early 2011.

Overall, inflation in Saudi Arabia and the UAE exhibit similar movements where inflation rates have increased from early 2005 and peaked in mid-2008, then decreased subsequently (Figure 4-2). The Divisia core inflation for both countries has been more stable than the traditional core inflation throughout the entire period. In the past couple of years, the volatility of the traditional core inflation has been more pronounced in the UAE, where the traditional core inflation stood above the Divisia core inflation from 2010 to 2011, while below the Divisia core inflation subsequently.

4.3.3 Constructing a Single Core Inflation Indicator for the GCC Area

The Gulf Monetary Council (GMC) is expected to launch a single currency that will be circulated in the Gulf area by 2015. However, the GMC has not yet determined the policy rule it will adopt for the Gulf area. For this reason, we carry our comparison between the alternative aggregation approaches under the assumption that core inflation indicators are utilized in the setting of monetary policy for the GMC. In this sense, we hope our core inflation indicators provide guidance to GMC policymakers when selecting which policy to implement.

While the GMC consists of only four member GCC countries, we carry out the empirical analysis over all GCC countries to provide broader insights about the price development and economic outlook in the Gulf region. We build the core inflation indicator for the Gulf area based upon two different monetary aggregation approaches: i) the conventional simple-sum monetary aggregates that are supplied by the GCC central banks, and ii) the Divisia monetary aggregates produced in Alkhareif and Barnett (2012). When using the simple-sum monetary aggregates, we define the traditional core inflation indicator for the Gulf area as:

$$\tilde{\pi}_t = \sum_{k=1}^{K} h_{kt} \left[log\,(\tilde{p}_{kt} e_{kt}) - log\,(\tilde{p}_{k,t-1} e_{k,t-1}) \right] \quad (4.11)$$

where h_k is the kth country's GDP share in the Gulf area. Since the GDP weights are considered ad hoc weights, this approach of aggregation violates aggregation theory and does not produce nesting of the multilateral or unilateral representative agent approaches [see, e.g., Barnett (2007)]. This aggregation method is unsatisfactory and inconsistent with index number theory. Therefore, we do not promote applying GDP weighted averages of inflation rates over GCC countries to produce a single inflation rate for the Gulf area. Instead, we propose an alternative core inflation indicator that is consistent with aggregation theory and index number theory. The Divisia core inflation indicator for the Gulf area is defined as follows:

$$\tilde{\pi}_t^D = \sum_{k=1}^{K} d_{kt} \left[log\,(\tilde{p}_{kt}^D e_{kt}) - log\,(\tilde{p}_{k,t-1}^D e_{k,t-1}) \right] \quad (4.12)$$

where d_k is the kth country's expenditure share of the Gulf union's monetary service flow.

The traditional inflation and the Divisia inflation along with their corresponding core inflation indicators for the GCC area are presented in

Figures 4-3 and 4-4, respectively. We estimate the alternative core inflation indicators for the GCC area using monthly data over the period of June 2004 to December 2011. In both cases, the core inflation indicators were below the Gulf inflation during the financial crisis—implying that a large portion of inflation during that period was driven by short-term factors and idiosyncratic shocks. Moreover, the core inflation indicators stand above their inflation indicator counterparts in the past year. This signals higher future inflation in the GCC area.

Table 4-1 reports short summary statistics of the alternative inflation measures along with their core inflation indicators. The means and standard deviations pertaining to the Divisia inflation indicators are higher than those for the traditional inflation indexes. These findings underline the fact that Divisia indexes not only provide a reliable measure of liquidity in an economy as they can approximate the unknown theoretical aggregator functions without errors, but also exhibit a stronger correlation to aggregate spending in an economy.[19] The standard deviation of our Divisia core inflation indicator is about 42% smaller than that of the Divisia inflation while this percentage is lower for the traditional core inflation as compared to the traditional inflation—suggesting that the Divisia indexes lead to smoother outcomes.

The correlation between our Divisia core inflation indicator and the Divisia inflation for the Gulf area stands at 97%, whereas the correlation between the traditional core inflation indicator and the traditional inflation is slightly lower (95%). This is an indication that the Divisia core inflation indicator tracks the Gulf inflation more closely than its traditional core inflation indicator counterpart.

The broad monetary aggregates are more correlated with the Divisia inflation indicator (between 78-83%) than with the traditional inflation indicator (between 70-74%). The correlation between the alternative monetary aggregates and the Divisia inflation indicator is on average 8.5% higher than those for the traditional inflation. The broad monetary aggregates have also a higher correlation with our Divisia core inflation indicator (between 83-85%) than with the traditional core inflation indicator (51-56%). On average, the correlation between the broad monetary aggregates and the Divisia core inflation indicator is about 30.5% higher than the correlation for the traditional core inflation indicator. Since there is strong linkages between our Divisia inflation indicators and the broad monetary aggregates, using the Divisia indexes

[19] See Barnett (1980b) for a thorough discussion regarding the theoretical background of Divisia indexes. See Barnett (2012) for more information about the connections between Divisia indexes and other macroeconomic variables.

will provide more informative content about price dynamics in the Gulf area. As indicated by Barnett (2012), Divisia indexes exhibit stronger relation with other macroeconomic variables including inflation rates. Constructing the Gulf inflation based on Divisia techniques is indeed useful for the monetary policy in the GCC area.

By applying cross-sectional and intertemporal smoothing procedures to inflation series, we produce core inflation indicators that are more stable than the Gulf area's inflation measures. Indeed, our core inflation indicators, being free from short-term oscillations and idiosyncratic shocks, provide a more reliable measure about price development in the Gulf area. In this regard, we provide policymakers at the Gulf Monetary Council (GMC) with a useful tool to monitor the price dynamics in the GCC area and to make well-informed policy decisions.

4.4 Forecasting Inflation in the GCC Area

A major role of the Gulf Monetary Council (GMC) is to scrutinize and monitor the dynamics of key macroeconomic variables such as output, unemployment, and inflation. To avoid occurrences of price instability in the Gulf region and possibly evolving systemic risk induced by variations of inflation rates between GCC countries, the GMC seeks to closely monitor inflation. Forecasting inflation is essential to strengthen the monetary policy in the GMC. We believe that using properly weighted monetary aggregates such as Divisia monetary aggregates will lead to improvements in inflation forecasts for the Gulf area due to the following reasons. First, Divisia indexes are derived based on solid microeconomic aggregation theory foundations and they belong to the class of superlative index numbers defined by Diewet (1976), as opposed to the simple-sum indexes. It is essential for monetary policy to maintain an accurate measure of the total liquidity of the economy, since higher liquidity levels can lead to higher inflation rates. As a result, monetary policy is more likely to be effective in monitoring liquidity in the economy by using superlative index numbers, such as the Divisia indexes. Second, unlike the simple-sum indexes, Divisia indexes weights the monetary components according to their usefulness in transactions, thereby providing an accurate measure of liquidity. Divisia monetary aggregates, obtained by using a proper weighting system that is consistent with monetary aggregation theory, exhibit a stronger correlation than simple-sum aggregates to aggregate spending in an economy [see Barnett (2012) for more details].

In this section, we forecast inflation in the Gulf area by using the bivariate direct forecast model introduced by Cristadoro, Forni, Reichlin, and Veronese (2005). We investigate the predictive power in forecasting inflation of two different monetary aggregates, namely the Divisia monetary aggregate and the simple-sum monetary aggregate. We use the broad monetary aggregates in forecasting inflation since they exhibit strong link to the world economy [see, e.g., Alkhareif and Barnett (2012)]. We describe our forecasting procedure and discuss the results in the subsequent section.

4.4.1 Methodology: A Bivariate Direct Forecast Model

The h-step ahead forecast of the Gulf area's inflation is computed via the following bivariate linear forecast model:

$$\pi_{t+h} = \alpha + \beta(L)\pi_t + \gamma(L)m_t^i + \varepsilon_{t+h} \qquad (4.13)$$

where m_t^i is the nominal growth rate of the ith monetary aggregate, α, β and γ, and ε are the models' intercept, coefficients (within which L is the lag operator), and error term, respectively.

We use the inflation rates in (4.9) and (4.10) as our target variables to evaluate the forecasting performance from using the alternative monetary aggregates. More specifically, we use the two alternative monetary aggregates interchangeably to forecast the traditional inflation and the Divisia inflation in (4.9) and (4.10), respectively. As mentioned in the data section, the alternative monetary aggregates have been first log-differenced and seasonally adjusted to ensure their stationarity. For each forecasting model, we compute the Akaike (AIC) and Schwarz (SIC) information criteria to select the lag lengths from 13^2 different lags combinations of the right hand side variables. For both forecasting models, AIC and SIC information criteria selected two lags of inflation and m_t^i.

Using data prior to the forecasting period, we produce forecasts of inflation at the following horizons: $h = 3,6,12,$ and 24 months. To ensure that we use all available information efficiently, we apply the rolling-window technique in which we re-estimate the forecast models at each step while expanding the sample size.[20] To evaluate the usefulness of the two monetary aggregates in forecasting inflation, we compute the root mean squared error (RMSE) and Theil's U statistics to evaluate the forecasting model (4.13) for the alternative inflation measures, namely the Divisia inflation and the traditional inflation. For each model, let π_{t+h}

---

[20] See Binner, Bissoondeeal, Elger, Jones, and Mullineux (2009) for more details.

be the value of inflation at time $t+h$ and let $\pi_{t+h|t}$ be the forecast of inflation at time t. For each forecast horizon h, we compute the RMSE and Theil's U statistics as follows:

$$RMSE(model) = \left[T_h^{-1} \sum_{t=1}^{T_h} \left(\pi_{t+h} - \pi_{t+h|t}\right)^2\right]^{1/2} \tag{4.14}$$

and

$$Theil's\ U = \frac{RMSE(model)}{RMSE(random\ walk)} = \left[\frac{\sum_{t=1}^{T_h} \left(\pi_{t+h} - \pi_{t+h|t}\right)^2}{\sum_{t=1}^{T_h} (\pi_{t+h} - \pi_t)^2}\right]^{1/2} \tag{4.15}$$

where T_h is the total number of out-of-sample forecasts computed for the forecast horizon h.

4.4.2 The Forecasting Results

We evaluate the accuracy of the out-of-sample forecasts using the RMSE and Theil's U statistics for the different forecast horizons, $h = 3,6,12,$ and 24 months. In line with Binner, Bissoondeeal, Elger, Jones, and Mullineux (2009), we reserve the first half of our dataset for initial parameter estimations, while using the other half to evaluate our forecasts. Of course, the number of out-of-sample forecasts is not fixed, but rather varies corresponding to the forecast horizons. Since we have a total of 90 observations in our dataset, the number of out-of-sample forecasts is $T_h = 45 - h$.

Table 4-2 reports the results of the forecasting performance of the alternative monetary aggregates, namely Divisia M2 and simple-sum M2, over the period 2008:3 to 2011:12, for model (4.13) with the different inflation targets (i.e., the Divisia inflation and the traditional inflation). Our findings suggest that the Divisia monetary aggregates outperform the simple-sum monetary aggregates in forecasting inflation for all forecast horizons. As indicated in Table 4-2, the RMSE and Theil's U statistics for both models with different forecast horizons, h, are lower for the Divisia M2 than the ones for the simple-sum M2—implying the usefulness of the Divisia monetary aggregates in forecasting inflation.

The Divisia M2 dominates its simple-sum counterpart in forecasting the Gulf traditional inflation (Table 4-2). For each forecast horizon h, the RMSE and the Theil's U statistics associated with the Divisia M2 are lower than those for the simple-sum M2. Nevertheless, the RMSE and the Theil's U statistics for the random walk model of the traditional inflation are lower than those for the alternative monetary aggregates only at the forecast horizons $h = 3$, and 6. As indicated in Table 4-2, the Theil's U statistics for both monetary aggregates exceed one and hence the Theil's U statistics for the random walk model is smaller.[21]

The discrepancies between the alternative monetary aggregates' RMSE and Theil's U statistics are more pronounced for the Divisia inflation forecasting model than for the traditional inflation. At each forecast horizon h, the Divisia M2 provides more accurate forecasts of the Divisia inflation than the simple-sum M2. For example, for the longest forecast horizon $h = 24$ in the Divisia inflation forecasting model, the RMSE and Theil's U statistics for the Divisia M2 are about 12% lower than the ones for the simple-sum M2 (Table 4-2). In this regard, it is advantageous for the policymakers at the Gulf monetary council to use the Divisia monetary aggregates for monetary policy—as we have shown that Divisia M2 dominates the simple-sum M2 in forecasting not only the Divisia inflation, but also the traditional inflation as well.

4.4.3 Testing the Statistical Significance of the Inflation Forecasts

For our results to be meaningful, we evaluate the statistical significance of our findings. In order to measure the statistical significance of our results, we apply the testing procedure proposed by Diebold and Mariano (1995). Let f^{RW} be the inflation forecasts for the random walk (RW) model obtained by excluding the monetary aggregates from the forecasting model (4.13). Similarly, let f^{i} be the inflation forecasts for model (4.13), based on the monetary aggregate i. We test the null hypothesis that the forecast accuracy is indifferent between the RW model and the inflation model (4.13), against the alternative hypothesis that the latter has better forecast accuracy.

Mathematically, let $\varepsilon^{RW}_{t+h|t}$ be the forecast error from the RW model and let $\varepsilon^{i}_{t+h|t}$ be the forecast error from model (4.13) obtained using the monetary aggregate i. Let $L()$ be the squared forecast error loss function, that is, $L(\varepsilon_{t+h|t}) = (\varepsilon_{t+h|t})^2$. Hence, the loss differential between $\varepsilon^{RW}_{t+h|t}$ and $\varepsilon^{i}_{t+h|t}$ is defined as:

---

21 Our results are in line with those of Binner, Bissoondeeal, Elger, Jones, and Mullineux (2009) and Cristadoro, Forni, Reichlin, and Veronese (2005), for which random walk models can lead to better forecast outcomes in some cases. Nonetheless, in our study, Divisia monetary aggregates dominate both the random walk model and the simple–sum monetary aggregates in forecasting the Divisia inflation for the Gulf area.

$$d_t = L(\varepsilon_{t+h|t}^{RW}) - L(\varepsilon_{t+h|t}^{i})$$

The Diebold-Mariano statistic tests the null hypothisis of equal predictive accuracy:

$$H_0 : E\left[d_t\right] = 0 \tag{4.16}$$

Let

$$\bar{d} = \frac{1}{T_h}\sum_{t=1}^{T_h} d_t$$

and

$$V_{\bar{d}} = \gamma_\circ + 2\sum_{j=1}^{\infty} \gamma_j$$

where $\gamma_j = cov(d_t, d_{t-j})$.

The Diebold-Mariano statistic is defined as:

$$DM = \frac{\bar{d}}{\left[\frac{1}{T_h}\widehat{V_{\bar{d}}}\right]^{1/2}} \tag{4.17}$$

where $\widehat{V_{\bar{d}}}$ is the variance estimator.[22]

For the traditional inflation model, the Theil's U statistics for the random walk model are smaller than the ones for the alternative monetary aggregates only for the forecast horizons $h = 3$, and 6. Therefore, we do not compute the Diebold-Mariano statistic for the alternative monetary aggregates at the short horizon. However, the results for both monetary aggregates are statistically significant at the 5% level for the forecast horizon $h = 12$. For the forecast horizon $h = 24$, the results for the Divisia M2 and the simple-sum M2 are statistically significant at the 10% level with p-values equal to 0.0802 and 0.0612, respectively.

In forecasting the Divisia inflation for the Gulf area, our results for

---

[22] The Diebold–Mariano statistic is asymptotically normally distributed with zero mean and unit variance. See Diebold and Mariano (1995) for a more thorough theoretical discussion.

Divisia M2 are statistically significant at the 5% level, for the forecast horizons $h = 3,6$, and 12. At the longest forecast horizon $h = 24$, the result for Divisia M2 is statistically significant at the 10% level with a 0.0905 p-value. While the results for simple-sum M2 are statistically significant at the 5% level for the forecast horizons $h = 3,6$, and 12, the results are not statistically significant for the longest forecast horizon ($h = 24$), as the Theil's U statistic for the random walk model is smaller than the simple-sum M2 counterpart. The broad Divisia monetary aggregate always performs significantly better than the simple-sum predictors. As a result, the Divisia monetary aggregates provide useful information about the Divisia inflation in the GCC area.

4.5 Conclusion

Unlike the European central bank with the unified statistical system, known as Eurostat which provides area-wide data useful for the European monetary policy, the Gulf Monetary Council (GMC) has not yet produced any data for the Gulf area. Building on the work of Alkhareif and Barnett (2012), this paper provides inflation indexes for the Gulf area using alternative aggregation approaches: the traditional approach and the Divisia aggregation approach. The former approach uses ad hoc weighting (GDP share weights) to aggregate inflation across countries. However, this aggregation approach is disconnected from aggregation theory. Instead, we construct our inflation indexes by means of Divisia aggregation approach in which we apply the Divisia share weights. This method of aggregation is consistent with aggregation theory and statistical index number theory and hence it is more suitable for monetary policy [see Barnett (2007)].

Using the Generalized Dynamic Factor Model (GDFM) proposed by Altissimo, Cristadoro, Forni, Lippi, and Veronese (2010), this paper constructs core inflation indicators for the GCC countries. The merit of using the GDFM is that it permits us not only to separate common shocks from the idiosyncratic counterparts, but also to extract the long-term common component part from the common shocks—leading to smoother estimates. In order to construct the Divisia core inflation indicator, we use Divisia monetary aggregates as well as Divisia price aggregates from Alkhareif and Barnett (2012). As shown in that paper, Divisia quantity and price aggregates can serve as an "economic stability" indicator and hence Divisia indexes are useful in monitoring the economic stance. Therefore, Divisia core inflation indicator is in fact a reliable measure that can accurately gauge the outlook for price developments. The findings indicate that our core inflation indicators are smoother than the inflation measures published by the GCC central banks—as we eliminated the short-term oscillations and other idiosyncratic shocks from our inflation indicators. We also find that the Divisia core inflation indicators are more stable than the traditional core inflation indicators obtained by means of simple-sum monetary aggregates. Using the Divisia monetary aggregates along with the Divisia economic stability indicators such as assets' user-cost prices, dual prices, and aggregate user costs, as they provide useful information about the stability of the financial system, will indeed improve upon the smoothness of the core inflation measures.

To build the Divisia core inflation indicator for the Gulf area, we aggregate the Divisia core inflation indicators for the GCC countries based on the Divisia aggregation approach. Similarly, to construct the traditional core inflation indicator for the Gulf area, we aggregate the countries' traditional core inflation indicators using countries' GDP weights. Both core inflation indicators are more stable than the corresponding Gulf-wide inflation. Nonetheless, the improvement in the smoothness between the inflation measures and the derived core inflation indicators is bigger for the Divisia indexes than for the traditional counterpart. This is a clear indication that using Divisia indexes to construct core inflation indicators leads to a more stable result.

Finally, we examine the forecasting power of the alternative monetary aggregates in forecasting the GCC traditional and Divisia inflation measures. Our findings suggest that Divisia monetary aggregates have an edge over their simple-sum counterparts in forecasting both inflation measures, namely the Divisia inflation and the traditional inflation. Hence, we conclude that Divisia monetary aggregates are more useful in forecasting inflation in the Gulf area—regardless of the inflation construction method.

Table 4-1: Summary Statistics (Sample 2005:6 – 2011:12)

Statistics	Divisia inflation indicators		Traditional inflation indicators	
	π^D	$\tilde{\pi}^D$	π	$\tilde{\pi}$
Mean	5.51	5.40	4.99	5.04
Standard deviation	3.07	2.17	2.67	1.90
Minimum	1.94	2.46	1.70	2.03
Maximum	12.42	9.90	11.47	9.55
Correlation with Divisia M2	0.78	0.83	0.74	0.59
Correlation with simple-sum M2	0.80	0.85	0.70	0.51

Table 4-2: Forecasting Accuracy of Alternative Monetary Aggregates (2008:3 – 2011:12)

Forecast Horizon (months)	Divisia M2		Simple-Sum M2	
	RMSE	*Theil's U*	*RMSE*	*Theil's U*
(h)	Forecasting model (1): Traditional Inflation			
3	**1271**	**1.33**	1283	1.34
6	**1516**	**1.47**	1525	1.48
12	**1770**	**0.69**	1802	0.70
24	**1993**	**0.88**	2001	0.884
(h)	Forecasting model (2): Divisia Inflation			
3	**1695**	**0.84**	1760	0.88
6	**1685**	**0.84**	1714	0.85
12	**2135**	**0.89**	2190	0.92
24	**2709**	**0.90**	3062	1.02

Note: (1) For each forecast horizon, h, the Root Mean Squared Error (RMSE) for inflation forecasts is multiplied by 1000,000. (2) We use data from July 2004 to March 2008 for initial parameter estimations and for each h, we produce T_h

number of out-of-sample forecasts, where $T_h = 45 - h$. Finally, (3) Bold entries highlight cases of the best accuracy in forecasting inflation for each horizon h.

Figure 4-1: Annual Inflation Rates for the U.S. and the Gulf Area

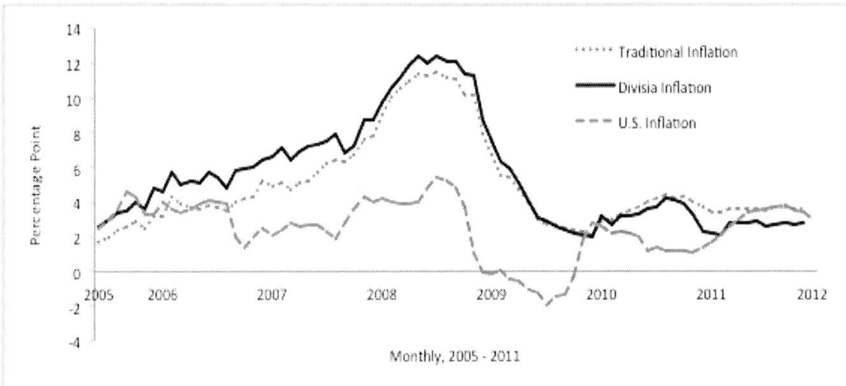

Figure 4-2: Annual Inflation Rates and Core Inflation Indicators for the GCC Countries

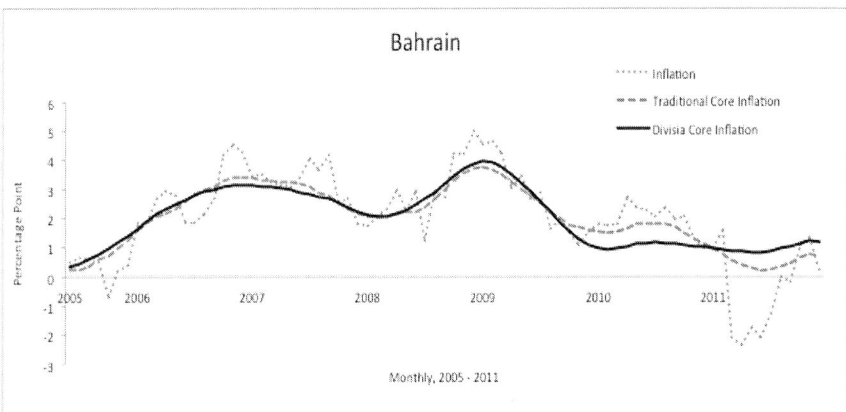

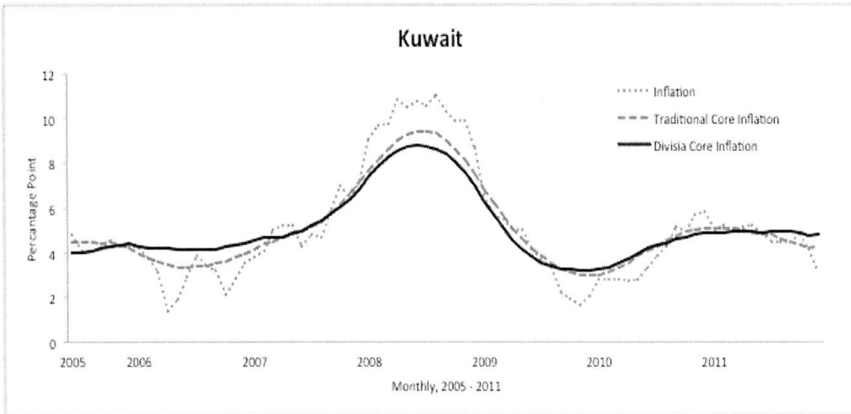
Kuwait
Inflation
Traditional Core Inflation
Divisia Core Inflation
Percantage Point
12
10
8
6
4
2
0
2005
2006
2007
2008
2009
2010
2011
Monthly, 2005 - 2011

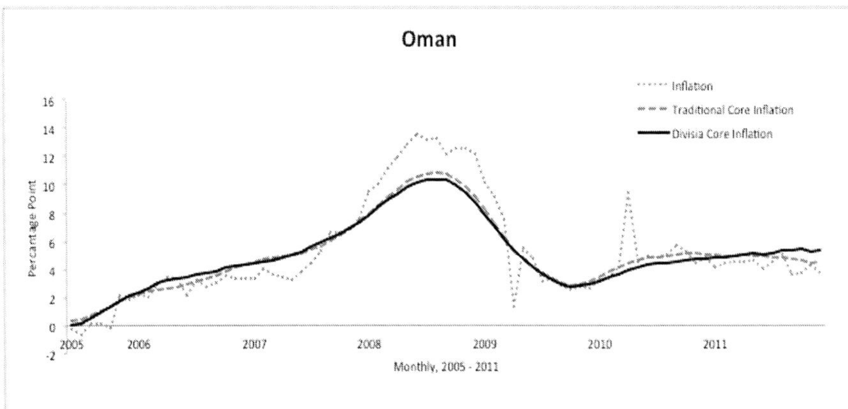
Oman
Inflation
Traditional Core Inflation
Divisia Core Inflation
Percantage Point
16
14
12
10
8
6
4
2
0
-2
2005
2006
2007
2008
2009
2010
2011
Monthly, 2005 - 2011

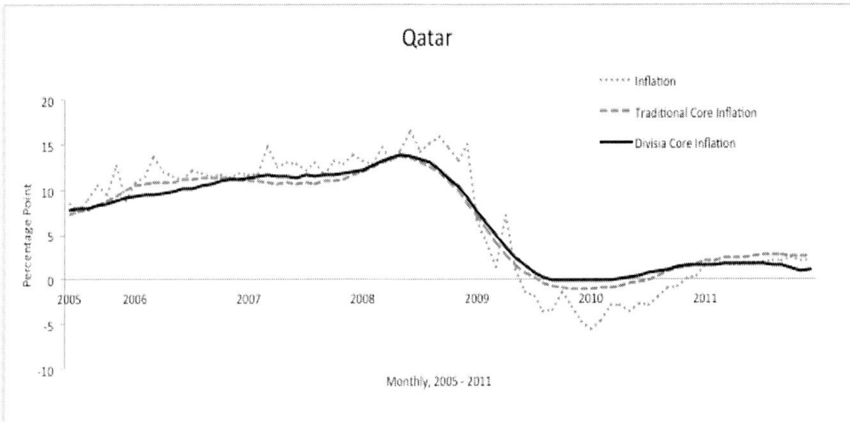
Qatar
Inflation
Traditional Core Inflation
Divisia Core Inflation
20
15
10
5
0
-5
-10
Percentage Point
2005
2006
2007
2008
2009
2010
2011
Monthly, 2005 - 2011

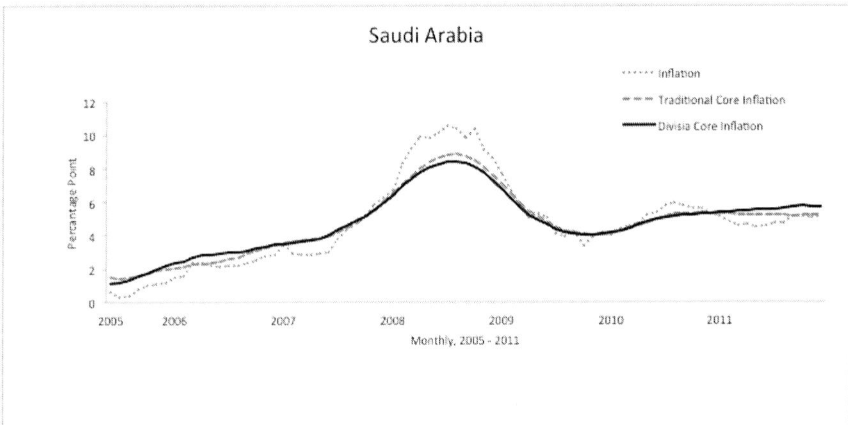
Saudi Arabia
Inflation
Traditional Core Inflation
Divisia Core Inflation
12
10
8
6
4
2
0
Percentage Point
2005
2006
2007
2008
2009
2010
2011
Monthly, 2005 - 2011

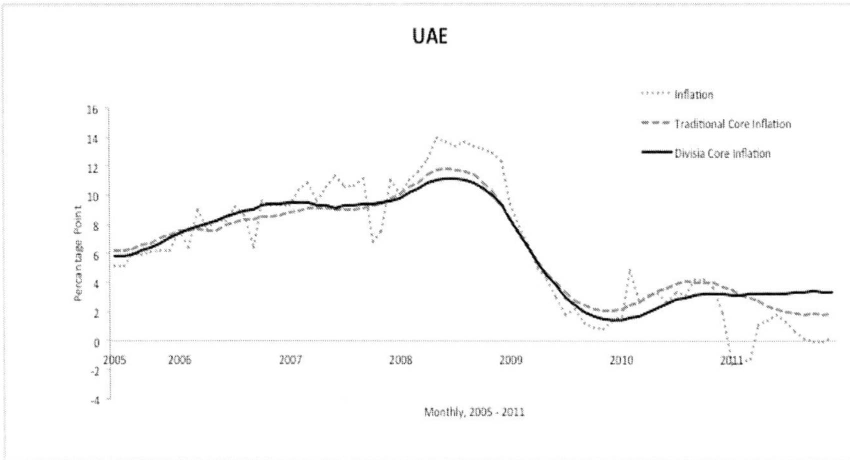

Figure 4-3: Annual Traditional Inflation Rates and Traditional Core Inflation Indicator for the Gulf Area

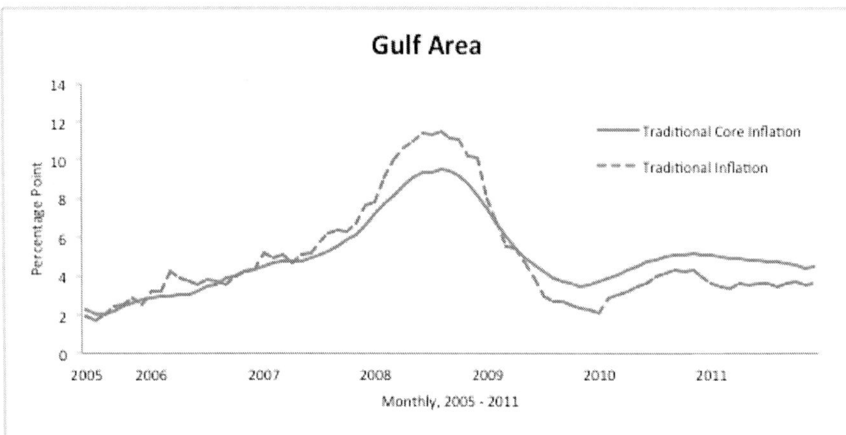

Figure 4-4: Annual Divisia Inflation Rates and Divisia Core Inflation Indicator for the Gulf Area

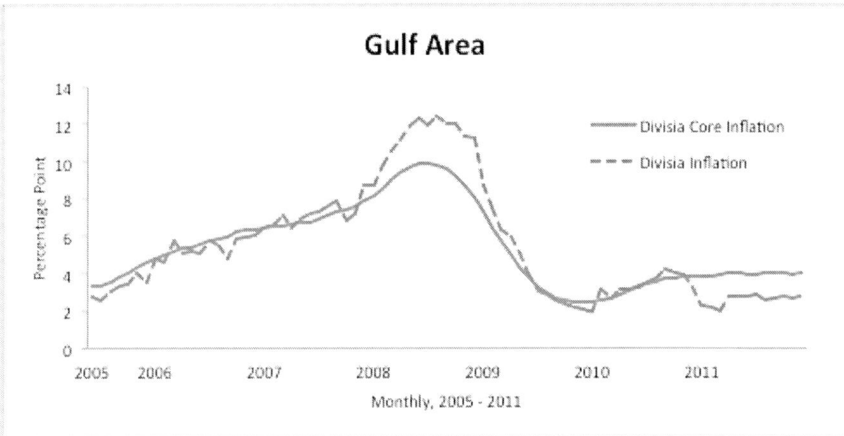

References

Alkhareif, R. M. , and Barnett, W. A. (2012). Divisia Monetary Aggregates for the GCC Countries. *In William A. Barnett and Fredj Jawadi (eds.), Recent Developments in Alternative Finance: Empirical Assessments and Economic Implications (International Symposia in Economic Theory and Econometrics, (Vol.22)*, *Emerald Group Publishing Limited*, pp.1-37.

Altissimo, F., Cristadoro, R., Forni, M., Lippi, M., and Veronese, G. (2010). New Eurocoin: Tracking economic growth in real time. *The Review of Economics and Statistics, 92*(4), 1024-1034.

Bai, J., and Ng, S. (2002). Determining the Number of Factors in Approximate Factor Models. *Econometrica, 70*(1), 191-221.

Barnett, W. A. (1980b). Economic monetary aggregates an application of index number and aggregation theory. *Journal of Econometrics, 14*(1), 11-48.

—. (1982). The Optimal Level of Monetary Aggregation. *Journal of Money, Credit and Banking, 14*(4), 687-710.

—. (2007). Multilateral aggregation-theoretic monetary aggregation over heterogeneous countries. *Journal of Econometrics, 136*(2), 457-482.

—. (2012). Getting it wrong : how faulty monetary statistics undermine the Fed, the financial system, and the economy. MIT Press, Boston

Binner, J. M., Bissoondeeal, R. K., Elger, C. T., Jones, B. E., and

Mullineux, A. W. (2009). Admissible monetary aggregates for the euro area. *Journal of International Money and Finance, 28*(1), 99-114.

Bryan, M. F., and Cecchetti, S. G. (1994). Measuring core inflation. In *Monetary Policy* (pp. 195-219). The University of Chicago Press.

Bullard, J., and Keating, J. W. (1995). The long-run relationship between inflation and output in postwar economies. *Journal of Monetary Economics, 36*(3), 477-496.

Christiano, L. J., Eichenbaum, M., and Evans, C. (1996). The Effects of Monetary Policy Shocks: Evidence from the Flow of Funds. *The Review of Economics and Statistics, 78*(1), 16-34.

Cristadoro, R., Forni, M., Reichlin, L., and Veronese, G. (2005). A Core Inflation Indicator for the Euro Area. *Journal of Money, Credit and Banking, 37*(3), 539-560.

Cristadoro, R., Saporito, G., and Venditti, F. (2012). Forecasting inflation and tracking monetary policy in the euro area: does national information help?. *Empirical Economis,* 1-22.

Diebold, F. X. and Mariano, R. S. (1995). Comparing predictive accuracy. *Journal of Business and Economic Statistics, American Statistical Association, 13(3),* 253-263.

Diewert, W. E. (1976). Exact and superlative index numbers. *Journal of Econometrics, 4*(2), 115-145.

Fischer, S., and Modigliani, F. (1978). Towards an understanding of the real effects and costs of inflation. *Review of World Economics, 114(4)*, 810-833.

Forni, M., Hallin, M., Lippi, M., and Reichlin, L. (2000). The Generalized Dynamic-Factor Model: Identification and Estimation. *The Review of Economics and Statistics, 82*(4), 540-554.

Forni, M., and Lippi, M. (2011). The general dynamic factor model: One-sided representation results. *Journal of Econometrics, 163*(1), 23-28.

Hallin, M., and Liska, R. (2007). The generalized dynamic factor model: determining the number of factors. *Journal of the American Statistical Association, 102*, 603-617.

Lim, C. H., Columba, F., Costa, A., Kongsamut, P., Otani, A., Saiyid, M., Wezel, T., and Wu, X. (2011). macroprudential policy: What instruments and How to use them? Lessons from country experiences. *IMF Working Papers*, 11/238 (Washington: International Monetary Fund).

Rich, R., and Steindel, C. (2007). A comparison of measures of core inflation. *Economic Policy Review, 13*(3).

Romer, C. D., and Romer, D. H. (1989). Does monetary policy matter? A new test in the spirit of Friedman and Schwartz. In *NBER Macroeconomics Annual 1989, (Vol.4),* MIT Press, pp. 121-184.

Romer, C. D., and Romer, D. H. (2003). A New Measure of Monetary Shocks: Derivation and Implications. *National Bureau of Economic Research Working Paper Series, No. 9866.*

Stock, J. H., and Watson, M. W. (2003). Has the business cycle changed and why?. In *NBER Macroeconomics Annual 2002, (Vol.17),* MIT press, pp. 159-230.

Stock, J. H., and Watson, M. W. (2010). Distribution of quarterly values of GDP/GDI across months within the quarter. Department of Economics and Woodrow Wilson School, *Research Memorandum.*

Stock, J. H., and Watson, M. W. (2011). Dynamic factor models. *Oxford Handbook of Economic Forecasting, Oxford University Press, Oxford, UK.*

Wynne, M. (1999). Core inflation: a review of some conceptual issues. *Working Paper Series (5), European Central Bank.*

JJ

0757 200 6014

Lang.